FINANCIALLY INTACT

Color Of Money Analysis
At

www.RonsFinancialPage.com

FINANCIALLY INTACT

Making Money is Easy, Keeping It is the Hard Part

RON VEJROSTEK

ISBN: 1511933062
ISBN 13: 9781511933063

DEDICATION

This book is dedicated to all the Vejrostek's who came before me and either directly or indirectly shaped me into the person I became.

"My dad and his parents"

TABLE OF CONTENTS

PROLOGUE

My philosophy of life is quite simple: "If we are not here to enjoy the ride and help each other along the way, then why the heck are we here at all?"

I think many people like their life's work and are basically content. On the other hand, I don't believe that most people actually *love* what they do. We all have something that we absolutely love doing. We love it so much that when we are doing that work, it is not work to us. For most people these are their hobbies, their avocations, because for one reason or another most people can't turn doing the "thing" they love into a sufficient enough income to make it the only work they do.

That's why retirement is so important. Most people don't get the chance to do what they really love doing for the majority of their life until they retire. And even sadder, many times people don't even get to pursue those activities then. Almost all hobbies have a certain cost associated with them. At the very least, if the hobby is not going to bring in any money, then the funds for everyday living must come from other sources.

Nothing makes me happier than to see people succeed in whatever endeavor it is that they wish. On the other hand, nothing makes me angrier than to see people getting ripped off, and unfortunately it happens every single day. You are going to read stories in this book about people who made one small, poor decision, aided by someone who wanted to get their money, where the result affected them for years and sometimes for decades.

We are in the middle of a major battle. On your side, you have yourself and hopefully a couple of trusted advisors. (Your advisors don't have to be financial professionals, just someone who really cares about you.) On the other side, there are a multitude of people who do not have your best interests at heart, and their only goal is to make your money their money.

The third chapter of the "Art of War" written by the great Chineese general Sun Tzu, states: "It is said that if you know your enemies and know yourself, you will not be imperiled in a hundred battles; if you do not know your enemies but do know yourself, you will win one and lose one; if you do not know your enemies nor yourself, you will be imperiled in every single battle."

Your best chance of staying financially intact is to be educated. This book is my attempt to help you recognize who your potential enemies are (there are more than you think) and to help you recognize their methods for getting into your pockets. You may look at some of the chapters in this book and decide that individual topics might not apply to you because of age, income bracket, or education, but I ask you to reconsider. Although you might be right at the moment, the information can nevertheless be of help to someone else you know, perhaps your parents or grandparents or your kids or grandkids.

This book was written to help you and those you care about, and it is my deep desire that it accomplishes that task.

INTRODUCTION

The great American middle class. According to U.S Census statistics, approximately 8% of American households have an income of more than $150,000 and about 41% of American households have an income of less than $40,000. That leaves 51% in the great American middle class. Now I know that a family of four trying to live on $41,000 is actually a poor family, but on the other hand a household of one living on $39,000 is actually in the middle class. The percentages then basically work themselves out and are about as stated.

Just a chance. That's all I want for most middle class Americans to have. Just a chance at achieving their dreams and getting the opportunity to do what they truly want to do and what they were born to do. I am one of the luckiest people in the world because I have gotten to do exactly what I wanted to do and love to do for the last 20 + years. Don't get me wrong, I am also a middle class citizen and I work very hard. Ten and twelve hour workdays are not uncommon, but I'm living the life I always wanted. I want every American to know what it feels like to live the life you always wanted.

The problem is that it takes money to do that. I don't care if what you want is to help teach children to read at a school you can walk to, you still must have money to pay your bills. We as middle class citizens have to work most of our lives at a compromised level, meaning we may enjoy our work but it is not our perfect life's work. That means most people don't get to live their dream life until they retire, but too often even that doesn't occur, because we don't accumulate enough wealth during our working years to fully relax and do everything we want in retirement or before. We work hard all our lives and we can make a lot of money, but it's hard to accumulate enough when we are constantly bombarded by people and organizations that are trying to take money out of our pockets and into theirs.

This book addresses many of the pitfalls that besiege us along the way and how to avoid or protect ourselves against them. The goal is to help us all stay Financially Intact.

Chapter 1

LEGAL

"... and justice for all"

Our pledge of allegiance is a promise to ourselves, for we are America. The United States is a geographical landmass, but America is us. "Justice for all" should mean all of us, not just the wealthy or those accused of crimes who can't afford an attorney. It should also mean for all victims of any crime or breach of contract. The sad fact is 90% of Americans can't afford an attorney for most instances.

America, ever since its beginning, has had a bad habit of saying one thing but meaning another. Our first official document, the Declaration of Independence, states "all men are created equal." But its definition of men must have meant "all white men." Fortunately, they did not use those words. At that point in time, many of the founding fathers believed in slavery, and, of course, women were not recognized as equals and allowed to vote until August 26, 1920, almost 150 years later. I say fortunately because the choice of those words "all men" opened the door so that eventually the wording could be challenged to mean all human beings. To this very day, politicians and the general public don't seem to agree on many terms. How often have we been promised "no new taxes," yet within just a couple of years we are paying more to the government because it instituted new fines or fees? It's all the same to us; if we are paying more money to the government, no matter what terminology they use, it is still a tax to us.

The "... and justice for all" phrase is extremely important for the context of this book. When most of us hear that phrase, the first thing that comes to mind is the Sixth Amendment. This amendment provides for a "speedy trial," a jury of our peers, and the right to a public defender for those who can't afford one. Well, that's fine for the accused and the criminals, but what about the victims? There are victim's rights, but the victims do not get all of the same rights as the accused. Ironically enough, when Congress finally passed a real victim's rights bill they called it the Justice For All Act of 2004. The rights that the law specifies are as follows:

1. The right to protection from the accused,
2. The right to notification,
3. The right not to be excluded from proceedings,
4. The right to speak at criminal justice proceedings,
5. The right to consult with the prosecuting attorney,
6. The right to restitution,
7. The right to a proceedings free from unreasonable delay, and
8. The right to be treated with fairness, and respect for the victims' dignity and privacy.

The rights listed above are for federal criminal cases. Most states also have victim's rights laws but, of course, there are still flaws and, as far as I am concerned, there are some rights that make no sense at all. For instance, the accused has the right to a speedy trial, however they also have the right to waive that right. The victims should also have the right to a speedy trial and should be able to override the accused's right to waive that right. Number 7 above says "free from unreasonable delay" but does not define that phrase, so I ask, what is reasonable about a

2 year delay? The accused as well as the convicted are given three nourishing meals a day, free television, no utility bills, and free medical and dental care. The victims don't have any of those guarantees, at least not until they become totally destitute and end up on welfare.

Let's go back for a minute to the "speedy trial" concept. In Colorado, on July 20, 2012, a gunman entered a theater, started shooting, and killed 12 people and injured 70 others. As of January 2015 this case still had not gone to trial. It is painfully obvious that the man accused is guilty. I refuse to put his name here and give him any more notoriety. The point is the victims and their families need to at least try to put this behind them and move on with their lives. How is it anywhere near fair to them that a few lawyers can delay this case for 29 months or more? I'm fairly sure public defenders have been assigned, and I sure would like to know how much they have been paid over the past 29 months. I think it should be mandatory that those fees be made a public record. If the public knew that answer, they would probably be demanding that this case go to trial now.

The problem with most laws is that they are written by lawyers. Federal laws are written by Congress and, on average, 40% to 45% of representatives and senators are lawyers. Now to quote Thomas Jefferson, "If the present Congress errs in too much talking, how can it be otherwise in a body to which the people send one hundred and fifty lawyers, whose trade it is to question everything, yield nothing, and talk by the hour?" My humble opinion is that laws are written, on purpose, in such a way that they can be argued about over and over again, almost indefinitely. Deep down, I believe that a lawyer's first loyalty is to his profession and the perpetuity of the profession. The best way to make sure that all lawyers have plenty of work is to write laws in such a way that there are always at least two ways to interpret the law by, of course, at least two different lawyers. I further believe that lawyers work so hard to protect criminals because this clientele is their best source for future income. Like any other business, repeat business is what they strive for. After all, who is most likely to commit a crime? Someone who has never committed a crime before or someone who has?

So you may be wondering, what has this got to do with staying financially intact? The answer is that I first needed you to understand that legal protection can hurt you two ways. It can hurt you because you do have it and it can hurt you when you don't. Here are two short stories about how protections can hurt you even when they are supposedly working for you.

A couple of years ago I was dealing with an issue with another party. Things were proceeding but I wasn't quite getting the results I was hoping for, nor were things moving along as swiftly as I would have liked. So as luck would have it, along with the fact that this matter was public record, a law firm that specialized in this particular specialty called me and offered their services. Although the caller said he was an attorney, he was basically the salesman for the firm. Of course, he sold me a bill of goods by touting the firm's experience and their normal results. I checked them out and thought I was making a wise decision.

So I paid them a retainer of $1,500, and they said they could probably finish the matter in 30 days, considering that I had already been working on the problem. Thirty days went by and I got a bill wanting more money. I called to ask for an update and all they said was that they were working on it and that they were no further along than I had been on my own 30 days earlier. Obviously, I asked them why they wanted more money and requested an accounting of how the retainer had been spent. Then I started getting upset that I was being charged $17 to $30 for phone calls that either got busy signals or where they left a short message. They had gone through the entire $1,500 in one month and had not accomplished a single thing. So now with $1,500 less in my arsenal, I fired them.

A couple months later I met a female attorney at a networking event. Since I many times have to refer people to attorneys, I am always on the lookout for someone who is good and reasonable. We agreed to have lunch a few days later. At that lunch I described my recent experience. She explained how the big firms train their lawyers to get that first retainer, go through the money without accomplishing too much, and then request more money. On average, it is thought that clients will send in payments three to four times before the issue is resolved. Now, personally, I think lawyers are overpaid to start with (we will get into that later), and that's when they are actually doing their jobs. I am sure you can imagine what I think about them charging 3 to 4 times that amount.

The second story goes as follows. One of my clients is a married couple who didn't trust lawyers, but we all knew they needed a trust because the husband was in the middle stages of Alzheimer's. Now, I am not a lawyer or any kind of expert on such matters, but the couple was older and they figured I had a better chance of understanding the attorney and re-translating his advice into plain English for them. So I went with them to the attorney's office. Like many attorneys, this guy was really long winded. He went on for about two hours selling himself and the kind of trust that he thought would work best. During the presentation he spoke at great length about how it was important to make the trust air tight and ensure the husband had no power to take money out of the trust. Considering the Alzheimer's and the things people sometimes do when they have this terrible disease, it was important to protect the assets from lawsuits and make sure the trust owned the couple's assets.

As we were getting to the end of the consultation, all of a sudden the lawyer acknowledged that most people have a problem with giving up total control of all of their money. His solution was to put in a clause that would allow the husband to access $8,000 per year for any reason. I looked at the wife to see if this was registering with her, but she just had a confused look on her face and didn't seem capable of voicing the obvious question. So I asked the lawyer how that made any sense, considering he had just lectured us for an hour about how the trust had to be air tight. I told him that it seemed to me that after closing all the doors he had just opened a window, especially since he was picking such an arbitrary number.

He replied that since it was under $10,000 it was a minor amount and would be okay. I noted that even in a best case scenario this could allow a creditor to win a judgment of $8,000 per year, and considering that Alzheimer's can take as long as 10 to 15 years to end a person's life, this could eventually amount to a lot of money. And that would be the best case scenario. The worst case would be that another lawyer could argue that the $8,000 figure is arbitrary and that all or more of the assets should be accessible. I asked the lawyer, if that were to happen would he defend his work for free? We got the expected answer that he would not, that a case like that would require extra billing for his time. After that answer, I flatly told him that I thought he was only adding the clause to potentially create extra income for himself at a future date. The client agreed with me that it made no sense and the clause was left out. The wife later thanked me and said that it was exactly why she was glad to pay me to be there. She knew something didn't quite sound right or make sense, but the lawyer had worn her down with his two-hour presentation. The point once again is, in many cases, a lawyer's first priority is to their own pocketbook and to the promotion of their own profession.

As we can easily see from the two examples, even though you have an attorney who is supposedly on your side, it can still be detrimental to your wealth. Make no mistake, we have to fight every step of the way to keep our money in our own pockets and stay financially intact. On the other hand, not having an attorney or legal help is just as dangerous and maybe even more so. Take the last example. Think of the ramifications had the trust not been executed and the husband had "escaped," taken the car, and caused an accident?

Everyday people like you and me use attorneys primarily for what are called civil cases. A civil case is one that does not concern a crime as defined by the legal system. (Here we go again with saying one thing but meaning another.) Some actions are subject to both criminal court and civil court. Probably the most famous case where that occurred was the O.J. Simpson trials. On average, civil cases have to do with one party suing another to recover damages for such things as a breach of contract. As I was writing this chapter, I have obviously been looking up legal definitions. Most of the definitions describe how criminal cases involve actions that affect the "state," which I suppose can be defined as society in general.

So the nagging question that has plagued me for about five years now is: why has no one from Wall Street gone to jail, not only for what they did to our economy back in 2008 and 2009 but indeed to the entire world economy? There have been a couple of civil cases and huge fines assessed because of those cases, yet somehow Wall Street firms have escaped any criminal charges. We talk a lot more about this subject in the chapter on Wall Street. One has to wonder if the amount of money a person has and is willing to donate to the lawyers (lawmakers) has anything to do with how the laws get determined as to whether or not a crime is considered criminal.

But as I said, the vast majority of the time we use lawyers for, or should be using them for, civil cases. It's therefore important to mention that, according to most websites, 90% of all civil cases never see the inside of a courtroom. Plus there are millions of other cases that don't ever actually get listed as a case with a court of law. Most, almost all, civil issues are settled with just a few letters or phone calls.

Even though we live in an outrageously litigious society, there would probably be even more civil actions, not necessarily court cases, if most of us could actually afford an attorney every time that we have been wronged. The sad fact is that most of us cannot afford to call a lawyer for many of those instances, because the potential legal fees could easily surpass the amount of restitution. And that brings us to the discussion of how and why lawyer fees are so high.

I guess the easy answer is that they can charge those kinds of fees because we allow them to by continuing to pay them. The legal industry has adopted billing everything in 6-minute intervals and that's why a 30-second text message gets billed at between $17 and $30, on average. I guess the obvious joke here would be that lawyers, although great with words and arguments, are terrible at math. Since there are ten 6-minute segments in an hour, lawyers apparently can't count past ten. Just like with texting, a lawyer's call to a busy signal or to a voice message also gets billed in 6-minute segments. Some firms, probably a lot of them, will charge you for every call. If a lawyer made three calls for you and they all happened in 6 minutes, you don't get billed for 6 minutes, you get billed for three calls as if each of them took 6 minutes. To make matters even worse, I have talked to some lawyers who used to work for big firms who were flat out taught that if they were on hold for one client, they should be billing for all that time. And while on hold they should also be texting or emailing someone else and billing for the time again.

According to May 2012 records from the Bureau of Labor Statistics, the average annual lawyer's salary was $130,880. This creates a bit of a dilemma for me. If the normal, average charge is $250 per hour, that works out to $520,000 per year. Now I realize one possibility is that the statistics specifically say salary; the study did not mention bonuses or other types of income they may also be collecting. However, that is still a substantial difference between $130,000 and $520,000, which is the equivalent of 2080 hours (a typical full-time job) at $250 per hour. So the more likely explanation is that most attorneys probably are not working 40 hours per week; therefore, they have to charge a lot more per hour for the hours they are actually working.

This leads me to the conclusion that we have too many lawyers. Since they all have to make a living they "invent" work to keep themselves in business and then, as already stated, they overcharge for the work they just invented. Of course, they have their fellow lawyers in the state and national lawmaking bodies writing ambiguous laws to help them stay in business. I have heard so many horror stories from clients that it just becomes sickening. One of my clients told me that when he and his ex-wife got divorced, they had agreed to an amicable resolution. It was, according to the two of them, a non-contested divorce but the lawyers stretched it out to two years and collected thousands of dollars in fees.

As part of the proof for some of the things that I have mentioned above, I offer you this copy of a lawyer's bill. Notice how a single text cost $50.

LEGAL

Invoice

Date	
10/31/14	

Bill To:

In reference to:
Investigation of

Date	Description	Hours	Rate	Amount
10/20/14	Meeting with	1.3	250.00	325.00
10/23/14	Meeting with	1.2	250.00	300.00
10/24/14	Phone calls with	0.3	250.00	75.00
10/24/14	Text with	0.2	250.00	50.00
10/27/14	Texts with	0.2	250.00	50.00
10/27/14	called	0.1	75.00	7.50
10/29/14	Phone call to	0.1	250.00	25.00
10/29/14	Phone call with	0.5	250.00	125.00
10/30/14	Phone call with	0.3	250.00	75.00
10/30/14	Called left message	0.1	75.00	7.50
10/30/14	Texted	0.1	75.00	7.50
10/30/14	called	0.1	75.00	7.50
10/31/14	called	0.2	250.00	50.00

Total	$1,105.00

$50 for one text! Are you kidding me? I doubt seriously that it took more than a few seconds to type that message. I further doubt that the attorney took 5 minutes and 40 seconds to decide exactly what he was going to text. I also doubt that after he sent the text that he just sat there and twiddled his thumbs until the 6-minute period passed by. Most likely he made a phone call or sent an email to someone else and charged them for a full 6 minutes also.

Here is an amazing fact for you. Take a guess at which is one of the most popular degrees held by lobbyists? You guessed it, a law degree. The people trying to persuade the lawyers, who are the lawmakers writing the laws, are basically fellow lawyers. It's absolutely amazing how much money gets sucked out of the economy by a profession that produces nothing. My general opinion is that lawyers are basically masters at the redistribution of wealth, much like our tax system, which is covered in Chapter 4.

On the other hand, at times when you need a lawyer, you really need a lawyer. The time to find a lawyer is not when you really need one but rather before you need one. After all, rumor has it that you only get one phone call after being arrested. So it's not like you can get out a phone book and start shopping around for one after the fact. And when you need a lawyer, you need the right kind of lawyer. An attorney who specializes in real estate transactions probably wouldn't be your best choice to defend you for a traffic violation.

I searched law specializations online and found on the Princeton Review website a listing of 10 different specializations, but there were a lot of major areas that were not mentioned, such as family law, real estate law, and water law. It's important to have the right lawyer for the situation. So it's probably best to have access to a large firm that has quite a few of the specialties covered. Have you ever been in a law firm's room that they call their library? You will see they have hundreds of books. Just to give you the full scope of how many laws there are, the Library of Congress' website states that it is the home to 2.65 million volumes of law books.

We all know that lawyers write in "legalese" instead of everyday language. They use such terms and phrases as "legal description attached hereto and made a part hereof as exhibit...." If a lawyer were writing this book we would probably already be on page 40 or 50. I recently lost my brother, and shortly before he left us we had his will prepared. All we really needed and wanted it to say was, "I want Ron Vejrostek to be my personal representative when I am gone." It took 5 pages to accomplish that task. I am not complaining, but it always baffles me how wordy contracts of any kind can be. I don't know about you, but I don't know anyone who has actually read every single word of the closing papers when selling or buying a piece of property. The signing alone usually takes about 45 minutes. Can you imagine how long it would take to actually read all those pages?

Speaking of reading, I decided to try looking up just how many laws there actually are. Needless to say, I can't find that answer. So then I decided a good way to get an estimate would be to see how many law books there are in a major law library. That number was also almost impossible to determine. So the closest I could come was finding how many books there are in the Library of Congress. At 2.65 million law books, that's a lot of laws, a lot of interpretations. Interpretations: perhaps we have just stumbled across the key to why we actually do need lawyers. As the old saying goes, "perception is 90% of reality." What was once perceived as legal many years later becomes illegal because our perception has changed. A prime example of that would be slavery.

Once upon a time it was "perceived" that men could own other human beings and, therefore, it was legal. Perception changed and eventually a new law was written to make it illegal. Owning another human being was no more "right" in the 1400's than it is today, but it was perceived to be okay and so it was. Reality did not change, the perception did. But let's take that a step further, as the new law now meant that we had to define slavery. That was done through another law, basically the one that sets the federal minimum wage, and then we start to face new problems and questions. What is a fair work week and how much should be paid to people who work in excess of those hours? Where do we draw the line between slavery and being paid a fair wage? What are reasonable demands of an employee?

Perceptions and interpretations. This is why laws are written and rewritten and argued over and over again by attorneys. So let's now look at interpretations. Our country was founded on the principle of "freedom of religion" but seems to have migrated to "freedom from religion." The original thought was actually "separation of church and state." The original intent was that our government could not tell us what religion to belong to or not belong to and it could not discriminate against us because of our religious beliefs. At the same time, the government should not be told how to proceed with the business of governing by any religion or religious group. Times have changed. I can't believe the amount of time and money that has been wasted on arguments such as, should a copy of the Ten Commandments be allowed to be displayed in a court of law or is it okay to have a nativity scene on government property? However unpleasant, this is why we have attorneys: perceptions and interpretations.

So now let's bring this topic to how it relates to helping us stay financially intact. When we were much younger, we rented a duplex from a real witch. We were good tenants and we left the space spotless and expected our deposit to be refunded. About 2 months went by and we hadn't received our deposit back, so I called the woman and inquired about the deposit. She informed me that the place was not left in the condition that she had wanted it. Upon further questioning, I found her definition of clean meant that she expected us to move the stove and refrigerator and clean the floor underneath those two items, which were the only things she could find wrong with the way we left the apartment.

I looked up the law, because we were poor and couldn't afford an attorney. What I found was a law that said if a deposit is kept the renter must be provided written notice of the reason within 30 days. So I took her to court, and when she tried to explain to the judge why she wouldn't give us our deposit back, he quickly stopped her and told her that it didn't matter, because the suit was justified when she didn't abide by the letter of the law and inform us in writing within 30 days. We got our deposit back.

However, if there had not been that law, the argument would have turned to what is considered "acceptably clean." You can immediately see the problem here: two people have two different interpretations as to what is clean and what is considered normal wear and tear. I am sure these disputes happen all the time. I'm also sure most renters cannot afford to hire an attorney to help them chase after a few hundred dollars. Yet on the other hand, I am sure that somewhere in those 2.6 million law books there is a precedent that more clearly defines those two exact words. It is because of circumstances and events such as these that we do sometimes need access to an attorney, but we need access at reasonable rates that we all can afford. No matter how small or trivial the case seems to the rest of the world, it is important to us.

If you need proof as to how many disputes there are over terminology, go on the internet and look at reviews for just about any business. The old saying "one man's garbage is another man's treasure" demonstrates that people define terms differently. It becomes a problem when one person decides they have suffered a monetary damage from the actions of another. For example, having a lousy server at a restaurant doesn't make us happy but it doesn't cause us any real damage, whereas being served rotten food would cause us monetary damage if we were still expected to pay for it, because we did not get the value for our money that was due to us. I use online reviews a lot and am always amazed at how 5 people will think a place or product is great and 3 will think it the worst ever. I am sure a lot of it has to do with expectations, which basically are the same as perceptions.

The same thing goes for accidents and property damage. In addition to owning an object, a person also has an emotional tie to that object, so they value their property higher than what the general public might value the same object. Thus, another person may view that object as used and, therefore, will not want to pay the full replacement value as if it were brand new. I see this all the time, when people are claiming a charitable contribution on their tax returns. Taxpayers have to be constantly reminded that we can only use a price that would be appropriate if the item were purchased in a thrift store. The dining room table and chairs you paid $800 for 10 years ago is not worth that today. One would probably be lucky to sell it for $100.

Enter the lawyers, who are the arbitrators in most cases. They know what the law says and they also know what constitutes currently acceptable practices. They also do not have an emotional attachment to the case. Their principal weapon is words. It is their job to bring everyone concerned to an agreement as to what the current perceptions are and what the current interpretations should be. This, of course, is the exact reason there are lawyers for each side. And this is why we need an attorney on our side. Considering the sheer number of laws, as well as precedents set by previous court cases and opinions, we as laypeople don't even know where to start looking in those 2.6 million law books. As an example, I did a quick internet search for "settlement on a broken foot" and received about 703,000 results. We will never find an attorney who has read every legal publication out there, but once you find an attorney who specializes in the area in which you need help, they will know where to start looking to find the pertinent information.

Now that we have pretty well determined that there are definitely times when we need an attorney, our next problem to solve is: how do we accomplish this task at a reasonable rate or fee? I started this chapter stating that most Americans feel they can't afford an attorney, and for good reason. One of the problems we run into is that when two lawyers get together on either side of an issue, we have an immediate new problem. We now have two attorneys who know the longer the case drags on the more money they will make. So it is not uncommon for we laypeople to wonder, "Why is it taking so long to settle this case or come to an agreement?" Obviously, when we are asking that question, we are not looking at it from our attorney's point of view.

Over the years, I have recommended a lot of people to get legal advice, because that is something I do not and cannot do. I know when legal advice is needed, and many times I even know the answer, but without a law degree it would actually be illegal for me to give advice. I always wondered why there wasn't a company or an organization that could do for legal services what I and thousands of others have done for the tax preparation business. For instance, we prepare taxes and give advice for about half the price of the national franchises and often much lower than CPA firms. We set ourselves apart by doing the job well, but mostly by offering advice at reasonable prices. I can't tell you how many of my clients have come to me because another client recommended they should talk to me. Not meet with me simply to get their taxes prepared, but to talk to me.

Many times, advice is all we need to make a wise decision on many matters. We don't know if we actually have a case or not. We don't know what our legal options are. We don't know what the odds are of winning a case if we did decide to proceed on a legal basis. So there are probably times when we could have and should have proceeded but we made a poor decision because we lacked accurate information. There are also times when people did proceed when they probably should not have, but the lawyer they hired needed the business and convinced them they had a case. I have often thought, wouldn't it be nice to call an attorney with a quick question, without being afraid that it was going to turn into an hour-long conversation costing $250? After all, it's just one quick question and I simply want advice.

So why isn't there a business that offers legal advice at a reasonable rate? Why isn't there a firm that offers quick advice without having to go in for a "free initial consultation," which in reality is just a sales pitch?

I have been noticing lately that there are a couple of firms that are offering alternatives to the old standby "way of doing things". Of course, there are actually good lawyers out there also. It is our job to find an appropriate attorney that we can work with and who will work with us. There is at least one firm out there who charges a reasonable monthly fee to have access to most of their services and I was going to talk about them here but they decided they didn't want to be mentioned in the book because, "The content is very negative toward attorneys". I am also sure that there are other firms out there somewhere that are attempting the same type of fee for service plan. I certainly hope so. There is an old saying that says, "if it isn't broke, don't fix it". In my opinion the legal system is broke and needs fixing. That will only happen if we start demanding that we get our money's worth, which in turn will help us stay financially intact.

Chapter 2

IDENTITY THEFT

"Identity theft is a criminal offense. It occurs when a person knowingly transfers or uses, without lawful authority, a means of identification of another person with the intent to commit or to aid or abet any unlawful activity that constitutes a violation of federal law or that constitutes a felony under any applicable state or local law."

--*IDENTITY THEFT AND ASSUMPTION DETERRENCE ACT, 18 USC § 1028(A)(7)THEFT AND ASSUMPTION DETERRENCE ACT, 18 USC*

According to the U.S. Postal Inspection Service, identity theft is the fastest growing crime in America. They cite statistics that approximately 9.9 million Americans are affected per year in recent years, costing those victims roughly $5 billion per year. According to the U.S Census Bureau, as of 2014 we have a little over 115 million households. Put those two numbers together and we can see that approximately 1 in every 12 households becomes the victim of identity theft on a yearly basis. Now, of course, some households become a victim more than once, but basically this tells us that within 12 years every household in America would be affected by identity theft, giving credence to the saying, "It isn't a matter of *if* you will be affected but rather a matter of when."

Most resources will tell you that credit card theft or abuse is only about 19% of all identity theft cases. Identities are stolen for many other reasons: income tax refunds, medical prescriptions, welfare benefits, driver's licenses, and all forms of other illegal activities. The most common form of identity theft is actually when someone steals someone else's social security number, plus a few other pieces of information such as address and birthdate, and then proceeds to use that information for their own benefit. The benefit can be such actions as getting credit cards, renting an apartment, getting utility services, phones, or even buying cars. The thief then, of course, does not pay the bills, thus giving the person whose identity was stolen a bad credit record, which can take months or even years to straighten out and have their good credit restored.

The IRS reports on its own website that between 2011 and 2013 it stopped $50 billion in fraudulent claims. On the other hand, the following quote is from the U. S. Treasury Department's own report: "Undetected tax refund fraud results in significant unintended Federal outlays and erodes taxpayer confidence in our Nation's tax system. Our analysis of tax returns using characteristics of identity theft confirmed by the IRS identified approximately 1.5 million undetected tax returns with potentially fraudulent tax refunds totaling in excess of $5.2 billion. TIGTA estimates the IRS could issue $21 billion in potentially fraudulent tax refunds resulting from identity theft over the next five years." The report reference number is 2012-42-080 and was issued July 19, 2012.

Many of the fraudulent returns are done with real names and social security numbers, but the criminals file fast and early before the legitimate taxpayer files their true return. E-filing is great, but because of the speed at which everything happens, unless something looks out of line the IRS will issue the refund. It's not until the real return is filed by the taxpayer that the IRS realizes there is a problem. Of course, at that point in time the IRS has no idea which is the correct return and which one is the fraudulent return.

Identity theft doesn't always involve money from the victim. I heard the story of one man who got stopped for a minor traffic infraction. Once the policeman checked the driver's license, he informed the driver that there were several warrants out for his arrest. Fortunately the policeman suspected something wasn't quite right and gently took the man to the police station and helped him establish that the warrants were not actually for him but rather for someone who had stolen his identity.

Losing or having a single credit card stolen is bad, but in the grand scheme of things it is the least serious of the crimes. Most banks and credit card companies do not hold the victim responsible or liable, so it's mostly an inconvenience. Having your identity stolen and used for monetary reasons is much worse. When it affects your credit score it starts to affect your entire way of living. A poor credit score can stop you from obtaining credit and, therefore, prevent you from doing such things as buying houses, cars, and many other major purchases.

There are also less obvious ways that a bad credit score can and does hurt people. Some auto insurance companies pull credit scores and adjust premiums or even decline insurance if the scores are not high enough. People have lost employment opportunities because of poor credit scores and been turned down from being able to rent a home or apartment. As bad as all this is, even that type of identity theft is mild compared to a stolen identity being used by someone who has committed a crime.

The internet is full of horror stories about people who have been arrested because someone has stolen their identity and then committed a crime or perhaps several crimes. They have found themselves handcuffed and taken to jail, sometimes for a couple of hours and sometimes for a couple of days, and that's just the start of their problems. Many have been arrested more than once by different police departments or counties. To see if this is happening in your town or a major city near you, simply search for "false arrests due to identity theft" and add your town or state. You will undoubtedly find a few stories of people who have lost their jobs, their families, their self-esteem and even their homes, all because of identity theft.

There is a story of one man who quit a job as a retail salesman because he assumed those kind of jobs were plentiful and easy to get. Job interview after job interview went well, but at the last moment he would not get offered a position. After a while, in frustration he asked why he was not offered a position. The reply was that the results of a background check were not acceptable. After further investigation, he learned he had a criminal record that he knew nothing about. His wallet had been stolen a couple of months before he had quit his former position.

It would seem problems like this should be easy to fix, but that is not the case. With monetary identity theft you only have to deal with a couple of companies and 3 credit bureaus. However, once you have a criminal record and it gets into the computers of "information brokers" and different legal entities, it's almost impossible to remove all the traces of the incident or incidents. The information brokers sell the information to many other places, and believe it or not, they claim they don't keep track of everyone who has bought records from them. Even if they did, it doesn't mean that the companies who purchased the data will care enough to make a correction.

Once someone is accused of a crime, their fingerprints are taken and filed. This is frequently how police departments determine that the person they have in custody is not the same person originally arrested for committing the crime. However, getting the records expunged does not always go as planned for one reason or another. For example, the record of the crime you may have been arrested for might be cleared, but there could be other crimes in the system that do not get cleared out.

There are many ways for identity to be stolen. Many times it is not done by someone who is a habitual thief, but rather by someone who simply does not act appropriately to a certain set of circumstances. It could be someone finds a lost wallet or purse and then makes some bad choices. Often the identity is stolen and used by a family member. In such cases there really isn't much you can do to prevent it. After all, people don't lose their wallet on purpose. It's often just a bad set of circumstances and pure bad luck, such as a wallet falling out of a purse or jacket or being left on a counter at a store. On the other hand, many times the wallets or purses are actually stolen, and this is something that can be avoided. We have to remember that many crooks are both fairly smart and very patient.

As much as I hate to admit it, I once lost a debit card at a casino in Las Vegas on the night before I was to leave town. I really didn't need to withdraw cash, but I decided I would use an ATM and take out enough for my trip home the next day, to keep that money separate from the amount I set aside for gambling. Several circumstances led to my troubles. First, the person ahead of me was taking a long time, so I got impatient. Second, the ATM worked exactly the opposite of the one I'm accustomed to at home. Instead of returning my card first and then the receipt, it switched that order. Unfortunately, we are creatures of habit. I was used to getting the receipt last, so once I pulled it I walked away without thinking that my card was still in the machine. Two days later I realized I no longer had my ATM card and called the bank immediately. I learned from the bank that within 30 seconds of my transaction someone attempted to withdraw money from a savings account. I didn't have that card connected to a savings account so the bank could verify it wasn't me who made that attempt. A few seconds later the bank's records showed that a couple hundred dollars was withdrawn from the checking account. I asked how this was possible without my PIN number and learned that if the card has not been fully removed from the machine, a person can simply push it back in without having to reenter the PIN. Thirty seconds is all that was needed. Luckily, the bank said because of the circumstances it would refund my money. But the point I am making is that it only takes a few seconds, a slightly different set of circumstances from our normal routine, and lack of 100% attention to easily find ourselves in a losing position.

How do crooks get our information besides our giving it to them unintentionally? They can steal our mail before we ever see it. Sometimes they get it from our trash. And sometimes it may not be as random as you think. Enter computers and the internet. Although the internet can be, and is, one of our greatest allies, it can also be one of our greatest enemies. The internet is great in that it makes it much easier for us to monitor our bank and credit card accounts and even our credit reports. All these things can help notify us as quickly as possible when something is amiss. However, the internet is also full of information we might wish was not public knowledge.

So let's go back to stolen mail again for a moment. Let's say a bad person saw on Facebook that it's your birthday, so now they know the month and day but not the year. However, since it's your birthday, chances are you are going to be getting some birthday cards and odds are that someone will say something inside the card to the effect of "Happy 39th", so now the crook knows the year you were born. By going back to Facebook or other internet sites, they can obtain more information about you. It's also easy to find out when someone just had a baby. That tells a crook a social security card will soon be coming in the mail. I don't know exactly how they do it, but by the time my granddaughter was 4 years old we were getting phone calls from a credit card company, looking for her because she was behind on payments. Because there are not many people with our last name, they called my home on the chance that we were related. It took us quite a while to convince them that she was a 4-year-old girl who didn't have a credit card. In reality, someone had already stolen her identity.

Another really popular way that people steal other people's personal information is by remotely accessing our computers. While there are many ways this task can be accomplished, the sad thing is that we are the party most responsible for letting it happen. Way too many people use public wi-fi to check their email and even pay bills or check bank balances. However, if you turn your cellphone into a hotspot, then you can use your tablet or laptop more safely. A "hotspot" created by a cellphone works for just a very short distance, a few feet, and it is password protected, whereas public wi-fi covers a broader area.

I remember a TV news story during the last Olympics, where a reporter sat down in a café with public wi-fi. He had special software installed on his computer that would show when someone was accessing it remotely. In under a minute someone else, on the same wi-fi system, was taking information from his computer. We have really fooled ourselves into believing that we must conduct business at every possible opportunity. Believe me, if you can't do it safely, it most likely can wait.

In the next chapter we will be talking about scams and shams and explaining many of them in great detail. Because of the speed at which information can now be disseminated, it is of utmost importance that we take every step possible to protect our reputations, our credit worthiness, and our wealth. I hope this chapter impressed upon you that no matter how smart we are, it only takes a few seconds of being slightly inattentive for us to become the next victim.

Chapter 3

SCAMS AND SHAMS

*"In Africa, every morning a gazelle wakes up and
knows it must run faster than the fastest lion or it will
be killed. Every morning a lion wakes up and knows it
must outrun the slowest gazelle or it will starve to death.
It doesn't matter whether you are a lion or a gazelle,
when the sun comes up, you better be ready to run."*

--*AUTHOR UNKNOWN*

What is the difference between scams and shams? A scam is an illegal activity: someone gets your money or your identity and you get absolutely nothing in return. It is a criminal activity. A sham is where you do get something for your money, but what you receive is not worth anywhere near the value of what you paid or gave up for it. Shams are usually not illegal, however they are highly immoral. Throughout this chapter I am going to tell you about many of the most common scams and explain as best as I can all the details involved. You will see that many of these crooks have put a lot of thought into these scams, and they are designed to play on our weaknesses.

Whether we like to admit it or not, we all have weaknesses. Sometimes what we see as our strengths are actually weaknesses. For example, we might love to help people and to us that is a strength, but to a scam artist it is a weakness to be "played." You will see under the dating sites scam exactly how they take this particular strength and turn it into a weakness they can exploit. Do not skip this chapter thinking that you are too smart to ever get scammed! As we discussed in the previous chapter, it only takes a few seconds for us to lose when we are not at our 100% very best. Some scammers are out to steal our money, others are out to steal our entire identities. Our best defense is being aware of the many ways that we can be scammed.

As a tax professional I have in the neighborhood of 700 clients, and it is through my clients that I frequently learn how these scams work, because they have either gotten the calls themselves or know someone who has gotten the calls or the mail. From what I have learned from them, I am the messenger to help spread the word to all of you.

I know I keep repeating myself, but a lot of these crooks really are quite intelligent. They know that, for one, their story has to be believable and therefore must contain some truth. They also know that we humans are most moved to action by emotions, with fear being the number one emotion that elicits an immediate response. The interesting thing about fear is that it works both ways. We can be afraid of losing something but we can also be afraid of not participating in something good and missing out. The crooks also know that it's easiest to get someone's attention when they use a current piece of news or an event that people have an emotional tie to.

The very day I was about to start writing this chapter, I received an email from the IRS, talking about one of the very scams that I was planning to write about. The email contained issue number 2015-5 from the IRS newswire. It explains this scam perfectly, so I am including the entire issue here.

THE IRS SCAM
Phone Scams Continue to be Serious Threat, Remain on IRS "Dirty Dozen" List of Tax Scams for the 2015 Filing Season

WASHINGTON — Aggressive and threatening phone calls by criminals impersonating IRS agents remain near the top of the annual "Dirty Dozen" list of tax scams for the 2015 filing season, the Internal Revenue Service announced today.

The IRS has seen a surge of these phone scams in recent months as scam artists threaten police arrest, deportation, license revocation and other things. The IRS reminds taxpayers to guard against all sorts of con games that arise during any filing season.

"If someone calls unexpectedly claiming to be from the IRS with aggressive threats if you don't pay immediately, it's a scam artist calling," said IRS Commissioner John Koskinen. "The first IRS contact with taxpayers is usually through the mail. Taxpayers have rights, and this is not how we do business."

The Dirty Dozen is compiled annually by the IRS and lists a variety of common scams taxpayers may encounter any time during the year. Many of these con games peak during filing season as people prepare their tax returns or hire someone to do so. This year for the first time, the IRS will issue the individual Dirty Dozen scams one at a time during the next 12 business days to raise consumer awareness.

Phone scams top the list this year because it has been a persistent and pervasive problem for many taxpayers for many months. Scammers are able to alter caller ID numbers to make it look like the IRS is calling. They use fake names and bogus IRS badge numbers. They often leave "urgent" callback requests. They prey on the most vulnerable people, such as the elderly, newly arrived immigrants and those whose first language is not English. Scammers have been known to impersonate agents from IRS Criminal Investigation as well.

"These criminals try to scare and shock you into providing personal financial information on the spot while you are off guard,"

Koskinen said. "Don't be taken in and don't engage these people over the phone."

The Treasury Inspector General for Tax Administration (TIGTA) has received reports of roughly 290,000 contacts since October 2013 and has become aware of nearly 3,000 victims who have collectively paid over $14 million as a result of the scam, in which individuals make unsolicited calls to taxpayers fraudulently claiming to be IRS officials and demanding that they send them cash via prepaid debit cards.

PROTECT YOURSELF

As telephone scams continue across the country, the IRS recently put out a new YouTube video with a renewed warning to taxpayers not to be fooled by imposters posing as tax agency representatives. The new Tax Scams video describes some basic tips to help protect taxpayers from tax scams.

These callers may demand money or may say you have a refund due and try to trick you into sharing private information. These con artists can sound convincing when they call. They may know a lot about you.

The IRS reminds people that they can know pretty easily when a supposed IRS caller is a fake. Here are five things the scammers often do but the IRS will not do. Any one of these five things is a tell-tale sign of a scam.

The IRS will never:

- Call to demand immediate payment, nor will the agency call about taxes owed without first having mailed you a bill.
- Demand that you pay taxes without giving you the opportunity to question or appeal the amount they say you owe.
- Require you to use a specific payment method for your taxes, such as a prepaid debit card.

- Ask for credit or debit card numbers over the phone.
- Threaten to bring in local police or other law-enforcement groups to have you arrested for not paying.

If you get a phone call from someone claiming to be from the IRS and asking for money, here's what you should do:

- If you know you owe taxes or think you might owe, call the IRS at 1-800-829-1040. The IRS workers can help you with a payment issue.
- If you know you don't owe taxes or have no reason to believe that you do, report the incident to the TIGTA at 1-800-366-4484 or at www.tigta.gov.
- If you've been targeted by this scam, also contact the Federal Trade Commission and use their "FTC Complaint Assistant" at FTC.gov. Please add "IRS Telephone Scam" to the comments of your complaint.

Remember, too, the IRS does not use email, text messages or any social media to discuss your personal tax issue involving bills or refunds. For more information on reporting tax scams, go to www.irs.gov and type "scam" in the search box.

Additional information about tax scams is available on IRS social media sites, including YouTube http://www.youtube.com/irsvideos and Tumblr http://internalrevenueservice.tumblr.com, where people can search "scam" to find all the scam-related posts.

At the top of that article, the IRS talks about its "Dirty Dozen." We are not covering all twelve in the book, so if you would like to see the rest of the list, visit www.irs.gov and type "dirty dozen" in the search box. As I said earlier, knowledge is our greatest weapon, so I strongly suggest you read that article. It's an annual list that doesn't change much from year to year, but it's nonetheless worth reading and revisiting once in a while.

The worst part of the IRS scam is that, in many cases, maybe most, it is not Americans stealing money from Americans. The majority of these scams are being run by crooks outside of our country. I learned this fact from an official at the Colorado Bureau of Investigation. A couple of months ago, my household actually got the phone call twice in two days from the supposed IRS. My wife, already aware of this scam, called me at the office and gave me the number they called from and the number we were supposed to call to take care of this "problem." Knowing it was a scam, I decided to call the number to learn more about exactly how it works. When I called the number the first thing the person asked was, "What is your name?" I responded with, "What is your ID number?" I deal with the IRS on a weekly basis, so I know the first thing a real IRS employee always gives is their name and their ID number. The person on the other end once again asked for my name instead of giving me their name and ID number. I therefore told them I knew they were not the IRS and were scam artists. They told me if I wished to believe that it was my choice and I would pay the price, and they hung up on me.

Following this call I contacted my colleague at the Colorado Bureau of Investigation. When I told her I had their phone numbers for tracking and stopping this group, she gave me the bad news. The scammers make different numbers show up on our caller IDs that appear to be in the United States but aren't. She further informed me that the number I gave her had already been tracked and it actually first went through an exchange in Canada and then a second one in Russia. The Bureau could not track it any farther than that, so we don't know if the call actually came from Russia or yet another country. While some IRS scams may be organized inside America, our officials already know that the majority of the time this scam is initiating outside of the United States.

THE PUBLISHERS CLEARING HOUSE SCAM

As with many scams, there are a couple of versions to this one. One version informs people they have won a $500,000 prize, which in itself is a dead giveaway because Publishers Clearing House does not issue a $500,000 prize. The other version is actually much more believable, and because of that it catches a lot more people. As always, the crooks put a lot of thought into the process to make it as plausible as possible.

The more common version unfolds like this. The caller will tell you that he or she is from a firm hired to audit Publishers Clearing House records. During the audit they discovered that you had won one of the minor prizes, but they see no record of you having been notified and paid. They ask, "Did you ever get notified or paid?" And here is where the scammers really get good. They don't try to get any information from you. Instead, they tell you that you have to make two phone calls. The first call needs to be made to the Publishers Clearing House's prize distribution department in a particular state, and the area code they give you matches that state. The second call needs to be made to the IRS so that the taxes can be deducted.

The caller will tell you they have a special IRS contact who works with them to expedite awards so that they can get your money to you as quickly as possible. They remind the caller that the agent is in Washington D.C. and provide a correct area code. When the person makes the first call they are asked to provide their name and address and, for verification purposes, will be asked for more information, such as a birthdate. Another variation is that they will ask if you want direct deposit to get your money sooner and then, of course, they get your banking information. On the second call, when you think you are talking to an IRS agent, they get your Social Security number. The process works because they catch people off guard. According to Publishers Clearing House's website, they are aware of this scam and inform the public that they never notify winners by phone. So if you ever get one of these phone calls, hang up. You didn't win anything.

THE CREDIT CARD SERVICES SCAM

This is another phone scam that hurts many people because the scammers logically make it so believable. By the time you get this call, they already have most of your credit card information. The call comes from "card services," and the caller indicates they believe your card may already have been stolen or compromised. They can sound very sincere and convincing because they know what they are saying is 100% true: they are the ones who have actually stolen your card information. They will call you by name and ask to verify some details. They will tell you the type of card and recite the number and expiration date so that you can verify they have the correct account.

By now you are starting to believe the call is real. So at this point they ask if you have the card in your possession. If so, they next say you have to prove possession by giving them the 3 digit code on the back of the card, or else they will have to cancel the account. Because the caller knew all the other information, people tend to believe they are talking to someone who is trying to help them, and they freely provide that last piece of information. They will later find out someone fraudulently purchased all kinds of things by phone or through the internet. The real problem with this scam is that we do get legitimate calls of this nature at times. The best step is always to hang up and call your bank or financial institution directly to verify if they called.

Another frequent variation to the credit card scam is that you will get an email or a text message that your bank account with "XYZ" Bank has been compromised. They will use a local bank or credit union name that is prevalent in your area and use scare tactics by saying your account will be frozen until you call a specific number and verify your information. The reason I always know it's a scam is because they tend to name a bank and a credit union in my area with whom I don't have any account. This one happens so frequently that I am sure it is working to the scammer's benefit or they would move on to a new scam. The solution to both these scams is to thank the caller for the notification, tell them that for security reasons you will call them back, but instead call your bank directly. Do NOT use the number they provide to you during that phone call.

MEDICARE AND MEDICAL ALERT SCAMS

This is one of those scams where people have an emotional tie because of the way it's represented. The caller will tell a senior that because of "Obamacare" there are new Medicare benefits they may be entitled to. Now, the crooks know there has been a lot of negative publicity about how "Obamacare" has taken away benefits from Medicare recipients, so victims are often eager to learn if they are missing out on something. The scammer now starts going through a list of medical conditions, asking if the senior has any of them. As we all know, many seniors do have some kind of medical condition. They ask about diabetes, arthritis, COPD, asthma, bad knees or hips, and continue until they hit a likely condition. Once they find one, they match up a benefit that the person should be receiving for free. They then tell the person that they would like to get that benefit to them and can take care of it right now over the phone once the person verifies their Medicare eligibility. So they ask the person to read the number off their Medicare card. Unfortunately, that number is the person's Social Security number, and they have just unknowingly had their identity stolen.

The medical alert scam is also done by phone. To avoid it, you first need to know that neither Medicare nor Medicaid will ever pay for a medical alert system, which is a gadget with a button that a person can push if they need medical help. The scammer will say that a family member is concerned about them and has agreed to purchase a medical alert, but they ask you to verify the information and then ask for your credit card as a backup in case anything goes wrong with the other card. Once again, because the crooks have moved the victim to an emotional place, the person is not thinking with a completely clear mind. The easy way to avoid this scam, like the others, is to request the exact name of the company, then look up their number on the internet (do not take the number they give you), and call them back.

Sometimes people legitimately need to provide their Social Security numbers or Medicare number. The rule of thumb is to never give out your numbers to anyone who has called you. It's generally okay to provide this information when you have initiated a call to a known, reliable business.

THE FACEBOOK AND DATING SITE SCAMS

I get to hear a lot of stories because of the seminars I offer. One person came to one of my Scams and Shams seminars and, after hearing what I had to say, also came to the next one and brought a friend, because he thought that I needed to hear his story so that I could pass it on to others. The man was a divorced man in his late 40's or early 50's and had a profile on Facebook. A young, pretty girl asked to be friends with him and he accepted. Shortly afterwards, he received a private message from her telling him her sad story. She said she was the daughter of missionaries serving somewhere in Africa. Sadly, she said her parents had recently died in some kind of tragic accident. The new missionary who replaced them was not a good man and was mean to her (basically the Cinderella story).

After a few more conversations, she asked the man to send her a smartphone with a prepaid calling plan so they could talk directly. He agreed and sent one to her. They still mostly communicated by email though, because she claimed the phone service was too intermittent. She next went on to say that the new missionary was abusing her, and to get out of that situation she asked him to send several thousand dollars to allow her to get her papers, ship her few possessions, and buy a ticket to the United States and be with him.

He asked me what I thought. While it's possible all of that story was true, it most likely was not, especially considering the country it was coming from. So I asked him a couple of questions. Did the voice at all fit with the photograph he had of her? He said no and had asked her about it, but she claimed it was simply hard to get a good phone connection. I told him it was probably a scam, but if he wanted to make sure he could ask her to send an updated photo of herself using the smartphone. He thought that was a good idea. I haven't spoken to him again since then so I do not know the final outcome, but I do know that this is exactly how dating scams work.

Many of the dating sites are full of scammers. They browse through the listings and find someone who has a passion for something, let's say horses or dogs, for example. Then they build a profile matching the wants of the person they are about to scam. Next they make contact, detailing all the things they have in common (but you can bet they will not say they live in the same state as the soon-to-be victim). After they have become friends for a while, they let loose the scam. Let's say the person loves dogs. The scammer will make up a story about how they are trying to build a shelter and create a dog rescue center. They will tell the person that they have spent all their money on the legal work, or whatever, but now need money to build the kennels and they wonder if their new friend might want to help. People are bilked out of thousands of dollars every year by these types of scams.

As you can imagine, there are an innumerable number of variations to this scam. Sometimes the scammer will say their wallet has been stolen and they just need a loan of a couple hundred dollars. Sometimes they will say they need bail money because their ex showed up, a fight broke out, and both got arrested for domestic violence or disturbing the peace. No matter the story, the aim is to work their way into your heart and then into your pocketbook. According to my friend at the Colorado Bureau of Investigation, a large percentage of these scammers don't even live in the United States. Many actually work for our enemies and use the money to fund their operations and harm Americans living in their part of the world. So when any one of us falls for one of these scams, we are actually getting hurt twice.

Another dating site scam involves membership fees. Many sites allow you to join for free and browse profiles, but you can't communicate with others unless you upgrade to a paid plan. Given the number of profiles on the site, you figure it's worth the price for at least a month or two, and you use your credit card but you don't read the fine print. So now you start contacting other members and emailing them through the site. After the first month goes by, if the victim closely watches their bank accounts, they see that their credit card gets charged for 2 to 3 times the amount they thought they were paying to be a member of the site. When they call to complain, they learn that if more than 1 or 2 emails are exchanged with the same member an additional monthly charge is incurred.

According to the person who told me about this scam, he then contacted two of the women whom he had been corresponding with and asked them if he could use their personal email addresses to stay in contact, since the correspondence through the site was costing extra money. In both cases the women said they were not comfortable with giving out their real email address. The women may as well have said, "Are you crazy? Do you really think I was interested? This is how I make my money."

Are all dating sites part of a scam? Most likely not, so the best advice I can give is don't take short cuts. Take the time to read the small print before you provide your credit card information.

MAIL SCAMS
In this section we will cover scams that could come by either email or "snail" mail, aka U.S Postal Service. I offer you the following example of common email scams.

Attn: Beneficiary,

I am Rev Felix Awele Chairman of Fund Recovery Committee.

This is to bring to your notice that the Federal Government of Nigeria has mandated this office to recover all floating / unclaimed fund and transfer them back into the federal government treasury account.

In the course of carrying out this exercise, I saw your name and email among the list of people who have never receive their contract/ inheritance fund ($10.8M usd)

Please, I want to know from you the reason why you abandoned such big fund up till this time without any claim, I discovered that this payment file was abandoned for so long. It is quite unfortunate that you have not received your funds till now.

We, hereby apologize for the inconvenience and delay this may have caused you in the past not receiving your funds.

Meanwhile, you are advice to reconfirm to us your information below after reading this email to enable us proceed for your payment.

1) Your Full Name:
2) Your Mobile and Home Phone Number:
3) Your Complete Address:
4) A Copy of Your Identification I.D:

Your maximum cooperation will help us released your funds as soon as possible and please don't make any mistake while providing the requested information's to avoid payment error and wrong payment.

I shall await your swift response.

Best Regards,
Rev. Felix Awele
Chairman

Another example is as simple as this next one.

I have a charity offer for you, Please I need you to signify your interest by replying to this email (ahmedhassan99@qq.com). I will make more details.

I am sure the thought going through your mind at this moment is the exact same one that goes through mine every single time I see one of these examples: "Do people actually fall for this stuff?" Apparently they do or this scam would have ended years ago. There are dozens, probably more, variations of this scam. Some offer to deposit your money into your bank account, some offer to send it to you through a debit card, and all of them offer unreal amounts of money. They come from a variety of countries, including ones we might normally consider to be friendly like England, the Netherlands, or Germany. Crooks live everywhere, including right here in the good old U.S.A., although local scams generally tend to be more realistic and are more like shams. These scams will tell you that you are a beneficiary, or that you have won a lottery, or that it is money that really belongs to a widow or a charity but they will pay you a percentage if you will help them get the money out of the foreign country before it gets seized by that country's government. There are more sophisticated versions that are written by someone who is proficient in English, unlike the above examples.

The scams are sometimes portrayed as an investment opportunity. There used to be one going around that told the story of how the firm or company was trying to get gold out of a foreign country but that it took a lot in legal fees to accomplish the task. So what they were looking for were investors to help with the legal fees, and then those investors would get to share in the profits. They would proceed to say that they were sure they would be successful because they had done it before. That should have been the first red flag. If they had done it before, then why would they need financing for the new project? It can start fairly small, but as time goes on the scammers request more and more money.

I once knew a plastic surgeon who got suckered into one of these deals, because he asked me if he could get a tax write-off on the loss if he didn't get his money back. By the time it was all said and done, this doctor lost about $40,000 to $50,000. Because he kept pestering them on an almost daily basis, he did finally get some of his money back, although I know it wasn't any more than half. I am sure the scammer merely ripped off someone else to pay off the surgeon, the old "Ponzi scheme."

YOUR FRIEND IS STUCK IN A FOREIGN COUNTRY

You will receive an email from someone you know that says they are stuck in a foreign country and that their wallet or purse has been stolen. They will tell you different stories such as they need money to buy a new visa from the American consulate so that they can get on the plane which their ticket is for tomorrow. They are creating a sense of urgency so that you will react instantly without giving it much thought. Sometimes it goes the other way and they will say it will take a week to get their documentation and therefore they need money to live on for the week. They don't ask right away for you to send the money they ask you to respond to them so that it makes it look more like you are really communicating with them. You are not. They have broken into your friend's computer and they have gotten hold of their email list. They create a new email account with that person's name and that is the account they are communicating with you through. I received one of these once from a friend, unfortunately for the scammer, I had just talked to my friend the day before. The email stated that he was stuck in England and yet I knew less than 24 hours earlier, he was in Denver. So I called Dan and asked him why he didn't tell me he was going to England. Of course he asked me what the heck I was talking about and then I explained to him that his email list had been compromised and he had better send out a broadcast email to all his contacts letting them know that he was safe and fine and still in the states. If you don't know for sure call your friend, don't answer by email.

A much meaner variation of this is where a young adult calls an older individual claiming to be a grandchild. As soon as the older person answers the phone the scammer will say, "Grandma, I'm in trouble and I need your help." Of course grandma or grandpa will ask, "Julie is that you?" Now the scammer has a name to use and they will play it from there. The girls will be crying to help disguise the voice and the boys will say they have a cold or hangover or whatever. This one usually states that they are on school break or in another state visiting friends and they need money to get home. They usually only ask for a few hundred dollars and unfortunately this scam is very successful. The way to protect yourselves from this type of scam is to have a family code word. So that if anyone in the family does get such a call they will ask for the family code and if it is not delivered the scam is instantly recognized. This is another one of those places where things like Facebook can really work against us. Some scammers, rather than play the hit and miss game, will watch for posts of kids who are going on break or vacation and then they look up the family name and the call is made. It would probably be a good idea to tell family members to wait till they get home before they tell the world through pictures and words that they have been on vacation.

PUMP AND DUMP

Have you ever received a really nice looking piece of mail that claims it is now time to invest in a company that is on the verge of a great breakthrough? I get these quite often. More often than not, they concern a new gold strike or a new area where the company has found huge oil deposits. The pieces of mail are large, in full color, and anywhere from about 8 pages to 16 pages. They do present a fair amount of general knowledge about the industry and make the point that they are talking about a multi-billion dollar industry. Then they start making the case as to why their company is perfectly positioned to grab its fair share of those multi-billion dollars. The stock is usually selling at under $3 a share and many times under a dollar.

The companies usually do exist, but in most cases they exist for the sole reason of selling shares of stock. If you look up the stocks, you will almost always find that they are only a couple of months old. The company is formed and then they hire a public relations firm to pump up the price of the stock by creating demand. Once a few million shares have been sold and the stock has been inflated to about 3 times the original price, they sell their shares and all the new investors are left owning stock that is now valued at pennies a share and will never go back up. If these were really good deals, people inside the industry would have bought all the shares themselves. If you really want to take a huge gamble and be on the ground floor of an opportunity, find a local company with a great idea that is trying to expand. The odds are still against you, but at least you will know it is a legitimate company, making a legitimate effort at trying to be a successful company.

Closely related to stock scams are the phone calls that try to get you to invest in limited partnerships. These are not normally scams, just usually really bad investment choices. Limited partnerships have been around for decades, and we hardly ever see one that actually produces a positive return. Limited partnerships were first formed for the wealthy to use as tax write-offs. The original idea was that the investors would get most of their money back through tax savings, and then if the high risk venture succeeded, that was frosting on the cake. The problem is that these types of investments pay great commissions, thus salespeople started selling them to anyone who would buy one.

I know one unfortunate guy who has invested multiple times into limited partnerships and has never made a decent return. He has bought ones related to music albums, movies, oil drillers and even golf courses, but not a single one of them has produced a decent return. About the only person who makes money in a limited partnership is the general partner or partners. There are a few well established oil drilling companies that operate as limited partnerships, but they are the exceptions. Make sure you do your homework.

As you can see, there are literally hundreds of scams you can read about all over the internet. So if your intuition tells you to question a letter, email, or phone call, I highly recommend that you use the internet to see what you can find out about the person, the firm, or the offer that you are considering. A couple of the better, more trustworthy sites that I have found are Snopes.com and Ripoffreport.com. Of course, you can also search using any of the major web browsers. Sometimes you can even be surprised and find out that what you were skeptical of is actually true. Not often, but sometimes.

SHAMS

As mentioned in the beginning of this chapter, shams are not illegal even if we lose money to them, because they do not fit the definition of a crime by the government. Shams are produced by masters of language. They change or use words and phrases in such a way that they know the general public will mistakenly read one thing and yet get quite a different result from what was described.

Let me demonstrate just how easy this is to do, using a very simplified example. Let's take just four words and then change the order. "The dog bit Bob." We feel pretty sorry for Bob, right? Now let's change the order to "Bob bit the dog." We now have a different opinion of Bob at this moment, don't we?

So let's take this to a more serious, practical example. This time I am only going to change one letter in a total of seven words: "You are the winner of the drawing." By changing just one letter, the phrase now reads, "You are the winner to the drawing." The result is two totally different meanings. In the first phrase you are being told that you are actually the winner of a drawing, that you have indeed won something. In the second phrase you are merely told that you have won the opportunity to be in the drawing, which means you haven't won anything you didn't already have. But many times our minds don't make the distinction between the words we see.

To prove this point, please read the following sentence: "It deosn't mttaer waht oredr the ltteers in a wrod are, the olny iprmoetnt tihng is taht the frist and lsat ltteres are at the rghit pclae. The rset can be a tatol mses and you can sitll raed it wouthit a porbelm. Tihs is bcuseae we do not raed ervey lteter by itslef but the wrod as a wlohe."

This example makes a comeback on the internet every now and then, but it is helpful because it shows that we don't always read exactly what is written.

Shamsters, as we will call them here, use all types of tricks to get you to believe something that isn't exactly true. Take, for example, if you get a letter and the return address is three names and then the address, let's say something like Fullem Robem and Stickum. What is the first thought that crosses your mind? The letter is probably from a law firm, right, because it's about the only industry that uses multiple names for a business name. So before we even open the letter we assume that it contains information of an important or sensitive matter, especially since that industry rarely uses direct mail for advertising purposes. Shamsters use tricks such as these and many others.

Another example is "actual size not shown." They know that a picture is worth a thousand words, so what chance do four little words have against a picture? How about the ones where they send you a check for $1 or even $10 but on the endorsement line of the check is the fine print saying that you agree to participate in their offer and pay a monthly subscription fee.

Beware of anything that authorizes the direct, "guaranteed" transfer of cash. They do guarantee that you will win, but they never really say how much on the front page of the solicitation. The only amount they mention there is the "opportunity" to win an additional $4 million. The only way to see the fine print is to separate page 1 from page 2 and then look on the back side of page one. There, it finally tells you that the odds of winning anything over a dollar are 1 in millions, but your odds of winning a dollar are 1 in 1. In other words, the reason they guarantee everyone is a winner is because they give $1 to everyone who responds. And as to the $4 million, it is nothing more than a list of sweepstakes being offered by other companies (often called "prize procedure documents"). All you will receive, along with your dollar, is a report that tells you about legitimate (hopefully) sweepstakes and how to enter them, which is information you can find on dozens of websites for free. And once they get you to do this, they sell your name to every other shamster who is willing to buy it. Hence, in short order your mail box is filled with similar offers. They do this very quickly in hopes that if you fell for this scheme once, you will do it again before you catch on.

I have a client who, when he was younger, was actually quite sharp but has become more vulnerable as he gets closer to the end of his journey. He received a letter stating that he had won a VISA card worth $10,000 as a special promotion. It was free money, the card was preloaded with the money, and all he had to do was pay a $20 registration fee. His one great regret is that he doesn't have more money to leave to his children so he figured it was worth the $20 gamble, even though he was a bit skeptical. One week later he received 15 more "sham" letters, all on one day. Although the envelopes had different company names and addresses, the odds are that most of them are owned by the same people, considering the addresses were from neighboring towns.

Later, this man's daughter told me the rest of the story, and it's a cautionary tale of how a mild sham can turn into a major scam. Because her father had responded to a couple of the mailings and had included his phone number, he now started getting calls. One of the callers said he had won a $2.4 million lottery in Nevada (a state that doesn't have a lottery), but of course they required more information. He swears he did not give out his banking information, but as you shall see they did get it.

After a couple of phone calls, they told him he had to pay taxes on the lottery winnings before they could release the funds, but they were willing to help him with that process. They promised to deposit $9,000 in his account the next day but then he would have to withdraw $10,000 and send it to them. The next morning there was a $9,000 deposit into his checking account, although he later learned those funds actually came from his wife's IRA account at the same bank. Somehow, the scammers had gotten access to all their accounts at that bank. But the man only saw the $9,000 deposit, believed the caller was legitimate, and overnighted $10,000 in cash via UPS as instructed.

And it gets worse. A couple of days later, as his wife and daughter tried to get ahold of him by phone, the guy assumed it was the card company calling again and barked into the phone, "I just dropped it off at UPS, and I'm on my way home now." This led the daughter to begin unraveling the scheme. First, she took her father back to UPS immediately and retrieved the overnight envelope. Inside, there was $18,000 cash. As the daughter checked all the banking transactions for the previous month, she found that another $10,000 had been withdrawn. They filed a police report, started intercepting all the incoming mail, and changed the father's phone number. Altogether $20,000 cash was lost, and it easily could have been $38,000 or more if the daughter had not accidentally been tipped off.

I know everyone is thinking right now that they are too smart to ever fall for a scam like this and that may be true, but think of your parents or grandparents who grow more vulnerable as they age. They need to hear these stories, and we need to be aware of their cognitive abilities and, eventually, their financial affairs.

Another popular scam guarantees that you have won a preloaded VISA card with "up to" $10,000. They go on to say that it is your money, that it is not a loan or repayable. As always, the devil is in the details. On one small line it reads, "Upon receipt you can use for online purchases or even over the phone." Notice how it does not say that you can use it wherever VISA is accepted? This means you will be offered cheap merchandise with shipping charges so high they still make money. Or perhaps, once again, all you're going to win is $1 preloaded on your VISA card, often with an activation fee of a greater amount.

And then there are the offers from the psychics who see great things in your future and for just a small fee they will send you your very own special report that will tell you what your lucky numbers are and other kinds of information that will help you attract great wealth.

One very big sham to beware of will tell you a secret society has been observing you for quite some time, and because you are a very special person, they have now decided you are ready to receive the information that will change your life forever. Once you know the secrets that the society will reveal to you, you will be able to attract whatever it is in life you want: fame, fortune, love, glory, or whatever. All you have to do is respond and they will send you an important free report. They actually do send the first "report" free, but I use the term loosely because it is really a heavily loaded sales pitch to convince you to buy the book that reveals all the secrets. Last I heard, the book was selling for somewhere around $100. However, it doesn't end there. At the end of the book it tells you to stay on the lookout for another letter that will bring you the next level of details. And, yes, you guessed it, there is another book to buy. I know there is a stage 3 also, but I do not know if it goes on beyond that because I have never found anyone who has gone past stage 2.

As you can see, shamsters have absolutely no shame whatsoever. They will use whatever means they can find to convince you to act the way they want you to act. They will often bring God and religion into it, making you feel as if you are a bad person if you do not act. They will bring family and children into it, shaming you into action so that your children can live the life you never had. They will exploit every one of the "7 deadly sins," knowing most people are guilty of at least one of them. They will twist their lies in every way possible to appear as true. They all offer products that are not strong enough to stand on their own merits so they rely on deception to make a living. As we've all heard, "if it sounds too good to be true it probably is not true."

Shams come in all shapes and sizes. Some are promoted by very large companies or at least companies that appear to be very large. They also involve just about every type of asset you can imagine. They can involve real estate, stocks and bonds, land, water, and precious metals. A new one growing in popularity involves buying very small amounts of gold. There is not anything illegal about what they are doing because the buyers can get the gold they purchase. The problem is that they sell the gold for 40% to 50% higher prices than a person could buy it on the open market. Their sales pitch sounds very practical and logical, and a lot of people are buying into it even though their arguments are full of holes. Of course, it is a multi-level type company (even though they have an argument as to why that is the wrong term), and that's why they need the markup on the product they sell.

But here's the point. Any product is worth a certain amount of money. A good story does not make it any more valuable, putting it in a pretty box or any other kind of packaging does not make it any more valuable, and just because someone says it's more valuable doesn't necessarily make it more valuable. If someone won't sell you a product at a fair price, look elsewhere and never take anyone's word for what something is worth. Always do your homework and make sure you are getting your money's worth.

Scams and shams can be so very devastating. I would like to end this chapter with another story. I have as clients a married couple who, unfortunately, found me as a result of a scam. The husband received a phone call one day where the caller talked about a tremendous invest-ment opportunity that was paying around 6% per quarter (not per year) and paid monthly. The offer concerned the buying and leasing of office and computer equipment in California. He was skeptical, but after a few phone calls he agreed to make an initial investment of $10,000. After he received a few months of checks, the salesperson called back and offered him an opportunity to invest <u>more.</u> He sent in another $10,000. After a few more months of checks, the salesperson called with a final opportunity to invest before the fund was closed to in-vestors. The salesperson actually convinced my client to leverage his money and take a $50,000 second mortgage on his house to invest at a higher rate of interest. The month after he sent in the $50,000, the dividend checks quit coming and the salesperson skipped town. My client obviously didn't have that kind of money to lose.

The couple ended up having to sell their really nice house in an upscale neighborhood. Worse than that, although he had been retired he now had to return to work, which he did until he was nearly 80 years old, when another relative passed away and he inherited a fair sum of money. This caring couple lost a lot more than $70,000. They lost thousands of hours of quality time they were planning on sharing together in their retirement. They lost travel opportunities as well as the real estate appreciation they would have received on a higher priced house in a desirable neighborhood. The husband also lost the ability to trust anyone when it came to investing, and so they lost legitimate op-portunities to make a little more money.

That is why <u>I have a passion to help people stop losing their hard-earned money.</u> I want people to keep their money in their own pockets and stay financially intact.

Chapter 4

TAXES

"Nothing is certain except death and taxes."

-- Benjamin Franklin

I ncome taxes didn't exist until 1913, although the fight for an income tax started years before then. I'm not taking any sides here, I'm just telling the story as it happened. The Democrats had wanted an income tax for several years, and the Republicans were against it. Eventually, the Republicans thought they could outsmart the Democrats by proposing the law to impose taxes as an amendment to the Constitution. Their thinking was that Constitutional amendments had to be ratified by at least ¾ of the states and there was no way that the people would vote in favor of taxing themselves. However, since the tax was only to be 1% and affected only those who made more than $3,000 per year, the battle cry became "Tax the Rich." You see, back in 1913, $3,000 of annual income was substantial.

In 1913, the year it became law, only 358,000 returns were filed, which represented 2% of all the households in America at the time. This would only prove to be the first time that Congress would pass a law under the guise of "taxing the rich" but then let inflation and bracket-creep force a much larger percentage of people into the folds of those being taxed. Just 10 years later, due to high inflation and World War 1, 40% of American households were paying income taxes. That percentage decreased in 1925 with some adjustments, but by 1942 more than 36 million tax returns were filed, which actually exceeded the number of households. This was possible because of children still living at home yet working and, thus, filing their own tax return and because of single persons sharing apartments and filing more than one return from the same address.

The next time the government passed a law under the guise of "tax the rich" was in 1983, when President Ronald Reagan signed into law the 1983 amendments to the Social Security Act. Not too many people complained or fought it, because "The Commission" estimated that its proposals would affect only about 10% of Social Security beneficiaries. That was true for the first few years, but once again inflation created another bracket-creep, because Congress, to this very day 30 years later, has never changed the formula. In 2012, Social Security beneficiaries paid in a total of more than $45 billion in taxes on their benefits. In 2010, about 34% of all people who received Social Security benefits paid taxes on those benefits. Within a few years the percentage will easily exceed 50% of all beneficiaries.

If this history lesson has started to ring a little bell in your memory, it well should. When the Affordable Care Act (ACA) was passed, part of the bill created a new tax, although actually it is an extension and increase of an old tax. The ACA requires households that make more than $250,000 (about 2% of all households) to pay an extra Medicare tax of 3.8%. What the heck, it's just taxing the rich, right? I guess history really does repeat itself.

Since we just finished the chapter on shams, I'll bet you're thinking taxes have some characteristics of a sham. We are promised or told one thing and delivered another. When it comes to shams, our government shamsters are truly among the best. In this case, I am talking about our welfare system. It was sold to us as a way to make sure that people don't fall through the cracks. We believe that the system is there to help people and keep them from becoming destitute. In reality, it is built to ensure that poor people stay poor. If it were really there to help people, it would be a system that would reward them for working their way out of it. Instead, it is built so that if the family makes as little as $1 too much they lose ALL their benefits. They lose their health care, their food stamps, their day care and housing allowances. News flash: $1 is not going to cover any one of those items, let alone all of them. If we truly wanted to help these people, we would have a graduated system. In other words, once they make $100 over the limit, only $50 of benefits is taken away and when they make $400 over the limit only $250 of benefits is forfeited. Our government is forcing people to stay on welfare by not giving them a way out that they can actually afford to take.

This brings us back to what our tax system actually is these days. Taxes are supposed to be monies that the citizens pay to their government so that their government will provide them with certain general services and to keep the people safe. Although we do get that to a certain extent, our tax system is now more about redistribution of wealth than anything else. Allow me to repeat that: our tax system now is more about redistribution of wealth.

To help prove that point, I offer you some statistics you likely won't find anywhere else. But first allow me to share with you my view of the political parties so that you know where I stand. My view is that one party wants to get their hands on as much of my money as possible and give it to everyone who is poorer than I am. The other party wants to get their hands on as much of my money as they can and give it to everyone who is richer than I am. So no matter who is in power, my number one concern is protecting my pocketbook. If you are a middle class citizen you probably feel about the same way.

So back to the statistics. You will find many sites that tell you the top 5% of income earners pay about 30 percent of the federal taxes overall. They then proceed to describe other percentage groups. The problem with their figures is that they use gross income and gross taxes, not taxes actually paid. To calculate the taxes actually paid, you need to take the tax credits out. Of course, once a person grosses over $150,000 the credits start to disappear, and by the time you hit $250,000 almost all the credits disappear. So when we take gross income and look at taxes actually paid, you will find that the top 5% of income earners pay a little over 50% of all the taxes actually paid. The top 53% of income earners (those who have earned income of $50,000 and above) pay a whopping 92.6% of all the taxes actually paid. The statistical chart from which I derived these numbers is the 2011 tax statistics chart that can be found at: http://www.irs.gov/uac/SOI-Tax-Stats-Individual-Income-Tax-Returns.

But these numbers still do not give us an accurate picture, because they only include the credits that are used to offset taxes. On top of those, there are the portion of the credits that are refundable. This means that if you run out of taxes owed, the government will just give you the cash for any credits you qualify for. The biggest of these is the Earned Income Credit. In 2011 a total of $62 billion was distributed as cash through the Earned Income Credit, a full 6% of the total amount of taxes that were collected. No surprise this money is given to the bottom 47% who supposedly only pay 7.5% of the tax bill, but once you deduct the 6% in refundable credits they pay almost nothing. The Earned Income Credit is the epitome of redistribution of wealth, and we will talk more about it later.

I wanted you to have this background because so many people tell me that they don't mind paying their fair share of taxes. I believe that too, but no matter how little we pay in income taxes by using the rules they have given us, we are still paying our fair share. I also want to mention here that the wealthy, the ones who make over $200,000 (the top 5%) are not always rich people. Many times people fall into this category for only one year. Here are two quick examples. I had a client who received a third of a ranch, and unfortunately it was given to him before the other owners died, so he owned it at their cost basis. This meant that when he sold his share for about $300,000, almost all of it was taxed. Inheriting his share in the ranch would have worked more to his advantage. That particular year, he was considered "rich" and paid accordingly. In another case, a woman sold a duplex that had been fully depreciated because she had owned it for over 30 years. So when she sold it for more than $250,000, she was considered rich for that year and paid accordingly. Yet that property basically was her retirement plan, and the proceeds were a once-in-a-lifetime event.

In paying our fair share, we all pay a lot more than we realize because of hidden taxes that get passed on to us as consumers. This was encapsulated in a speech President Ronald Reagan made in 1975. I offer you a portion of that speech here.

"If people need any more concrete explanation of this, start with the staff of life, a loaf of bread. The simplest thing; the poorest man must have it. Well, there are 151 taxes now in the price of a loaf of bread — it accounts for more than half the cost of a loaf of bread. It begins with the first tax, on the farmer that raised the wheat. Any simpleton can understand that if that farmer cannot get enough money for his wheat, to pay the property tax on his farm, he can't be a farmer. He loses his farm. And so it is with the fellow who pays a driver's license and a gasoline tax to drive the truckload of wheat to the mill, the miller who has to pay everything from social security tax, business license, everything else. He has to make his living over and above those costs. So they all wind up in that loaf of bread. Now an egg isn't far behind and nobody had to make that. There's a hundred taxes in an egg by the time it gets to market and you know the chicken didn't put them there!"

So hopefully by now I have impressed upon you that, in order to stay Financially Intact, you must not lose your hard-earned money by giving too much of it to the government in the form of taxes. So let's move on from here and start showing some ways to lower your tax bills.

For some of you under the age of 60, you may at first feel that some of these ideas are of no importance to you at this time. I beg to differ with you. Even though it might not be a strategy that you can currently use, your parents or grandparents could at times benefit greatly. Sometimes when people get older they have a harder time actually understanding some of these concepts. You, being younger, can learn them more easily and help your family members. If you don't care if they pay the government more, thereby leaving you less in the end, then go ahead and skip over the parts that don't apply. Very, very few financial advisors teach these concepts, so you may want to hold onto this book and refer back to it later.

The first concept is tax deferral, which is a part of most tax-saving tactics. Tax deferral means that the tax that would normally be paid on current income is not collected until you actually access the earnings. This concept is many times misunderstood, in that many people think that if they don't take the earnings they will not be taxed. In the case of most financial products, this is not true. For example, if you automatically re-invest dividends from a stock or mutual fund, the investment company and the government consider those dividends to be cash. In fact, only a few products and circumstances are eligible for tax deferral, such as retirement accounts like IRAs, 401Ks, SEPs, etc. All annuities and cash value life insurance products maintain a tax deferred status, as do most U.S. Savings bonds. Another commonly used tax deferred strategy is actually depreciation.

So let's look at the power of tax deferral. The following chart shows what happens when we start with $1 and double our money each year. In the left column our money is growing tax deferred, and we don't pay taxes until the end. In the right column we pay our taxes each year as we earn the money. So, for the sake of example, the assumptions are that in both columns we are earning 100% on our money every year. The second assumption is that the amount of tax paid each year is 30% (basically 25% federal and 5% state).

As you can see from the chart, deferring the taxes makes a world of difference. Even if at the end we had to pay the highest possible tax rate of 47%, we would nevertheless accumulate $555,745. Which would you rather have, $40,000 or $555,000?

So how can we put this tool of tax deferral to work for us? There are actually several ways we will explore.

$1.00	$1.00
$2.00	$1.70
$4.00	$2.89
$8.00	$4.91
$16.00	$8.35
$32.00	$14.20
$64.00	$24.14
$128.00	$41.03
$256.00	$69.76
$512.00	$118.59
$1,024.00	$201.60
$2,048.00	$342.72
$4,096.00	$582.62
$8,192.00	$990.46
$16,384.00	$1,683.78
$32,768.00	$2,862.42
$65,536.00	$4,866.12
$131,072.00	$8,272.40
$262,144.00	$14,063.08
$524,288.00	$23,907.24
$1,048,576.00	$40,642.31

SCENARIO ONE:

In the first book I wrote in 1995, I showed a method I called "flow control." (At that time, I wasn't aware that the term would soon also refer to a particular male health problem!) But the term still describes a tax strategy perfectly, so I am going to stick with it. Here is how it works. Remember the story about the woman who sold her duplex for $250,000? Using her as an example, let's say she could earn a reasonable interest rate of 4% on that investment. After perhaps spending $10,000, she now has $240,000 left. We take the $240,000 times 4% and see that it would produce $9,600 in interest. She now has two choices. First, she can take the $9,600 in earnings and pay taxes on the full amount. Assuming a 25% federal tax rate plus 5% to state taxes, her total tax bill per year would be $2,880, leaving her with only $6,720 to spend. Her second choice is to split the proceeds into three buckets of money, each earning 4%. We would leave one bucket 100% liquid and we would put the other two into a tax deferred instrument called an annuity.

What we do at this point is take the full $9,600 out of bucket one until it is empty. During the years this is happening, she is only paying taxes on the money that bucket one is earning. Thus, in year one she will pay tax on only $3,200, and at 30% that's just $960. In this scenario, the woman will have $1,920 more in her pocket every year until the first bucket runs out of money. She would then have the choice of spending the money or saving it in a fourth bucket that she can use later to increase her income to make up for inflation. Some people balk at this tactic because they are uncomfortable spending their principal. However, the chart below shows that the base asset of $240,000 remains intact.

	Bucket 1	Bucket 2	Bucket 3	Total Assets
	Liquid	Annuity	Annuity	
Original Amount	$80,000.00	$80,000.00	$80,000.00	$240,000.00
Earnings	$3,200.00	$3,200.00	$3,200.00	
Distributions	-$9,600.00			
New Balance	$73,600.00	$83,200.00	$83,200.00	$240,000.00
Earnings	$2,944.00	$3,328.00	$3,328.00	
Distributions	-$9,600.00			
New Balance	$66,944.00	$86,528.00	$86,528.00	240,000.00
Earnings	$2,677.76	$3,461.12	$3,461.12	
Distributions	-$9,600.00			
New Balance	$60,021.76	$89,989.12	$89,989.12	240,000.00

As you can see from the chart, the asset value stays intact, at least until such time as the first bucket runs out of money, which takes 10 years. In that decade the woman will have paid $19,200 less in taxes, or a full 2 years of extra income in her pocket instead of the government's. If this strategy actually helps her pay fewer taxes on her Social Security income, then the overall savings can be even larger.

You may be thinking this looks fine but what is the woman's tax picture going to look like after the first 10 years? More good news as we now switch to a different strategy. Buckets numbers 2 and 3 have grown to $118,419 in annuities. We can't use the same strategy as bucket one, because when money comes out of an annuity as a withdrawal, the earnings come out first and then principal, which would put us back in the same boat we were in originally, tax-wise. So instead we switch to a strategy that takes advantage of an IRS rule referred to as 72T.

What Rule 72T says is that if money is taken out in equal parts over a period of time, then each payment is considered part principal and part earnings. So in this particular case, since our original amount was $80,000 and our new balance is $118,419, each payment would be considered 67.5% return of principal (non-taxable) and 32.5% interest earned (taxable). Once again the woman will be paying tax on only 1/3 of her actual income from bucket 2. And bucket 3 is still growing for future use. To use Rule72T, we have to do what is called annuitizing the annuity. The action of annuitizing is widely misunderstood by most people. I cover it more fully later in this chapter, but for now just know that, when done correctly, if the person (annuitant) dies before all the money is paid out, the heirs get the balance, not the insurance companies.

We use Rule 72T in many different cases, under many different circumstances. It can be used to reduce taxes paid on Social Security earnings and it can also be used to avoid the additional Medicare tax that some people might be paying because of the Affordable Care Act.

SCENARIO TWO:

When a person reaches age 70½, they have to start taking money out of their retirement accounts (a required minimum distribution). This can be from an IRA, 401(k), or any other qualified retirement account. Many people wish they didn't have to do this, but the government assumes that, as a retirement account, the money should be withdrawn and used for retirement. So in this scenario let's assume the taxpayer has about $250,000 in retirement accounts and an equal amount, another $500,000, in non-retirement accounts. Up until this time, the person has been using the earnings from the non-qualified account without much of a tax hit and is not paying taxes on their Social Security income. However, once they are subject to the required minimum distribution, they find that it puts them into a higher tax bracket and, thus, their Social Security earnings start getting taxed. This is more common than you may think. I have seen IRA distributions get taxed as much as 32.5% when a client was only in the 15% tax bracket the year before. If the person needs and wants the extra income from the required distribution, that is one thing, but if they don't there is a way to fix this problem.

At age 70½ the minimum distribution table tells us that we take the balance of the retirement account as of the previous Dec. 31 and divide that number by 27.4. So someone age 70½ with a $250,000 retirement account would be required to take a distribution of $9,124. Each year the divisor number goes down slightly and, therefore, the minimum distribution gets larger. To offset this, it's best to reduce other taxable income, which can be done by moving other money into a tax deferred account such as an annuity or Series E savings bonds or a single premium life insurance policy. Doing this allows "taxable" income to remain the same. In this particular case, the taxpayer would need to move about $250,000 to a tax deferred account. Sometimes it is not feasible to move that much, but any amount moved will help the person keep more money in their own pocket and pay less in taxes.

SCENARIO THREE:
Speaking of IRAs, they provide us with a wealth of opportunities to better control our taxes. Unfortunately, many people forgo the

opportunity to withdraw from their IRAs tax free because they are too focused on keeping it there until age 70½. I try to convince people to always withdraw IRA money whenever they can get it tax free. Many seniors, because of standard deductions and personal exemptions, or maybe even through itemized deductions, pay absolutely no income tax and could even earn a few thousand more and still not pay any taxes. Especially when you are a married couple, you can actually earn a pretty fair amount of money without paying any taxes.

Social Security only becomes taxable when all other income plus half of Social Security equals $32,000. If we take into account that the standard deduction for two people over the age of 65 is $14,800 and the two personal exemptions equal $7,900, that adds up to only $22,700 of the $32,000 threshold. We can still add to that figure $18,600 in Social Security benefits and the couple still would not pay any income taxes nor would any of their Social Security be taxed. That then becomes the magic number.

To get your own magic number, take all of your Social Security income and divide it by 2. Subtract that number from $32,000. The answer is the amount of additional taxable income you can earn without paying any income taxes. Let's say your answer is that you could earn up to $22,700 of taxable income, but you are only bringing in $17,000. That means you could take $5,000 out of your IRA, which is taxable income, and yet not pay a single penny in taxes. You might be saying, if it works now I can delay and it will work later too. Unfortunately, that is not true.

Eventually one member of the couple is going to pass away, and when that happens the tax picture changes drastically. The standard deduction drops by half and so does the personal exemption. As a result, the amount of income that can be earned without paying taxes drops by half to just $11,700. Although 1/3 to 1/2 of the social security income will stop when a spouse passes, the threshold from where Social Security starts getting taxed drops to $25,000.

My opinion is that we should never miss an opportunity to bring in taxable income, tax free. Many people think that if they withdraw money out of an IRA account they have to spend it. However, you can actually take that distribution and re-invest it back into the same type of product that it came out of. This strategy also helps later on, because it reduces the amount that you will have to withdraw to meet the required minimum distribution at age 70½. Otherwise, you not only may have to pay full tax on the required distribution but you may also have to pay tax on more of your Social Security income.

One other tool that can be used to control taxes through tax deferral are Health Savings Accounts (HSAs). These are discussed in the Insurance chapter, but I did want to mention that it is a tool that should be considered if you are trying to lower your taxable income.

There are many other ways a good tax accountant can help you find ways to reduce your tax bill. Notice I said a *good* tax accountant. In most cases that leaves out a lot of people who just prepare taxes but don't give advice about how to reduce your taxes.

Last year I was contacted by a married couple who did their own taxes using one of the popular software products. After they were done, the husband said he thought something was not right. So he asked his wife to have a professional review it. She took it to one of the big national franchise offices, supposedly one of the elite offices because it was one of the few that is actually open year-round. That person looked over the return and said he thought it looked right. She reported this to her husband, but he still felt something was wrong so he asked her to get another opinion. The wife then saw a CPA, apparently not one who specializes in taxes. The CPA reviewed the return and thought it was okay, so they signed it and sent it in. A few weeks later the husband told this story to a friend who happened to be a client of mine. My client suggested that they call me, and the wife set up a meeting.

In less than 5 minutes I asked her why there was no depreciation on their rental property. She told me the software asked the question, "Can someone else claim the depreciation?" She answered yes (because of a unique set of circumstances) and so the software didn't allow the deduction. Unfortunately, the software didn't ask the obvious follow-up question of whether or not someone else actually did take the deduction. I have no idea how the national franchise firm missed it, outside of the fact that in general they overcharge and underperform. The CPA also missed the mistake, and I can only assume he specialized in some other form of accounting. The bottom line is the couple was missing a several thousand dollar deduction, which was worth more than $1,000 in taxes that they would have paid unnecessarily. The happy ending to the story is that I amended that year's return for them as well as the two previous years and helped them get thousands of dollars in refunds.

Try to work with a tax advisor who actually knows their material and works to help people pay the least possible, not only in the current year but also in future years. Not all CPAs specialize in taxes. Many of them only do taxes along with the other work they do (corporate audits, etc.) because it is, in their view, quick easy money. The same goes for many attorneys who prepare taxes. I actually know a couple of them who prepare taxes and charge a lot, yet they are nowhere near experts in the area. As for the big national franchise firms, you must realize that more often than not you will be working with someone who was just recently trained to use the tax software and is probably getting paid $9 to $12 per hour. Considering how much they charge for their services, you may find this surprising. But that is how they can afford to pay rent for a full year even though they actually use the space for about 3 months.

There are a variety of strategies that can be used to help people reduce their tax burden. Some of them make only a small difference and others make a huge difference. One of the other strategies that can make a big difference is taking advantage of the 0% capital gains tax rule. This rule was originally written to be in effect for tax years 2008-2009-2010 only. However, Congress has extended it through 2015. Because it could go away at any time, it is best that people take advantage of this tax law as soon as possible. If you are married and filing jointly and your total taxable income is less than $95,500, or if you are single and your total income is less than $41,300, then you will be able to take advantage of this *temporary* tax break. If your money is positioned in such a way that you can control where your taxable income comes from, then if you are married filing jointly you can literally bring in thousands of dollars of capital gains completely tax free. I had one client capture $37,000 in capital gains and not pay a single penny in taxes on those gains. Most people can't quite accomplish this task because too much of their income comes from pensions or wages or other income that can't be temporarily reduced, but most people should be able to bring in tens of thousands of capital gains in tax free because of this law.

Allow me to show you how this works and then give you a few tips on how to best make it work for you. If you are in the 15% tax bracket, your capital gains tax rate will be 0%. For a married couple filing jointly, the 15% tax bracket extends all the way to $74,900. That threshold is for ***taxable income NOT total income,*** meaning the number that is actually taxed after deductions and exemptions. So for a married couple, as long as your total gross income is less than $95,500 ($74,900 [the top of the 15% tax bracket] plus $12,600 [the 2015 standard deduction] plus $8,000 for the two personal exemptions), you can take advantage of the temporary capital gains rule. If your taxable income is under $95,500, then the difference is the amount of capital gains you can bring in without paying a single penny in taxes. For example, if you have $80,000 of gross income, then you would be able to bring in $15,500 of capital gains totally tax free ($95,500 - $80,000 = $15,500). If you have itemized deductions that exceed the standard deduction, you have an even larger opportunity.

There are only 4 exceptions of capital gains that are not eligible for this tax treatment:

1. Corporations cannot take advantage of this rule. It is for individuals only.
2. Sales of collectibles.

3. Qualified small business stock.
4. Recaptured depreciation (from rental properties or other "listed" property).

So now comes the creative part. There are no other restrictions, so everybody should be doing everything they can to take maximum advantage of this huge tax break. There is nothing in the rules that says you can't sell an asset, such as a stock or mutual fund, take the tax free gain, and then re-buy the exact same investment back the very next day. That way you are basically getting a double tax break. For one, you get to capture your gain tax free, but just as importantly, you get to now reset your basis in that investment. So the next time you sell that investment you will have a lot less gain that is taxed.

There are also ways that you can maximize the amount of the gain that you can bring in tax free, such as: If you normally take more than your required minimum distribution, you could take just the minimum, allowing for more capital gain income. Also, you could maximize deductions to get over the standard deduction or do inevitable repairs or upgrades to a rental unit, or if you own a small business you can buy equipment now that you know you will be needing in the near future.

Of course, the other way you can reduce taxable income is to put some of your assets into tax deferred instruments, thereby reducing your current income. The bottom line is: if you are sitting on gains in property, rental properties, second homes, stocks, bonds, or mutual funds, you need to be working with an expert to make sure you take maximum advantage of this tax break.

As you can see, there are a lot of ways to reduce taxes in any given year. They can't always be used every year, but certainly at times. Sometimes people will only claim the standard deduction but then they have an exceptional year of one sort or another. Perhaps they had a lot of medical expenses and find that they will be itemizing. In a case like this, they should put as many other deductions into that year as they can, and a good tax advisor will suggest that they get any other medical visits done that are feasible in the same year, such as dental work or vision wear.

Another strategy is to have two years' worth of charitable donations booked to the current year. If you normally donate several thousand dollars per year to a favorite charity, you can make this year's donation as usual but also give next year's donation before December 31, to record both years of charitable deductions in the same tax year. I have some clients who donate a lot on a yearly basis so I have them use this strategy every other year. In other words, every other year they take the standard deduction and during the other years they itemize.

I know there are stories about how someone took the same information to 30 different tax preparers and ended up with 30 different results. As bad as this sounds, it truly is no great surprise. Many of the tax laws are not exactly black and white and therefore are interpreted by different preparers in different ways. Here's an example: if you have two jobs, your mileage from job one to job two is a deduction. But if you are running a small business out of your home and you work on it every night, is your home business considered your second job, thereby making your commute home every night a legitimate deduction? Some preparers would say yes, others would say no. Depending on how literally you take the wording of tax laws, a case could be made for either answer. That is why there is a tax court that stays very busy hearing cases of opposing interpretations.

The point is you should have someone to work with who will look out for your interests and work with you to take every deduction that is allowed. I guarantee you there is not a boxed tax preparation software that will tell you after you finish your return, "By the way, if you took a little less out of your IRA next year, you wouldn't have to pay tax on your Social Security benefits."

Before leaving this topic I would like to make one other point. The national franchise firms like to brag about how they get Americans back more refund money than anyone else. But a refund is simply a return of money that you have paid. The big franchises take advantage of the people who really need their "refunds." As noted earlier in this chapter, the bottom 47% of taxpayers pay very little in taxes because they obtain a lot of money through the Earned Income Credit, which gives back money to those who don't make much. But these so-called refunds aren't truly refunds, they are giveaways. In my opinion if these companies are going to advertise the great amount of money they help their clients get, they should tell it like it is and advertise that they help redistribute wealth by helping the government give away more money than everybody else.

If you want to stay financially intact, you need to align yourself with someone who can actually help you plan to pay fewer taxes. Merely making sure that you get all your deductions is not planning. There are thousands of preparers who can accomplish this task. True planning is helping you know in advance that you will be lowering your tax bill for years to come. There are many good tax accountants out there, but with the immensity of the tax laws they tend to specialize. Some are great at personal taxes, some are proficient in corporate taxes, and then there are other specialties. So you need to find someone whose knowledge fits your needs.

Chapter 5

INSURANCE

I t's a wonder we have any money left at all after paying taxes and insurance. After all, we're bombarded with health insurance, life insurance, auto, homeowners, umbrella liability, flood, cancer, critical illness, long term care, and let's not forget extended warranties. On top of those, if you own a business there are errors and omissions, liability, crop, and livestock insurances, among others. Of all of these, health insurance is probably the most confusing and difficult to choose the right plan for your needs. Before we move into a discussion of a few types of insurance, let's first just talk about the concept of insurance, which basically comes down to the diversion of risk. As such, and as much as we might dislike it, insurance is a necessary evil.

The concept of diverting risk can be traced back thousands of years. A written record of this can be found in the Code of Hammurabi, which was written somewhere around 1700 BC. Ancient merchants practiced "spreading the risk" by having several caravans or several ships or boats, so that if one was lost or attacked only a portion of their total shipment or inventory was lost rather than the whole. Personal insurance is more recent, yet even it has been around for over a thousand years. The earliest proof of personal life and health insurance can be found in the early

Roman times (around 600 AD), where societies of craftsmen joined together in what they called "benevolent societies." These were formed to
take care of members' families and funeral expenses when the member
died. This idea was carried on and expanded by the guilds of Europe
in the Middle Ages.

Eventually, life insurance as we know it today came about in the late
1700's. Health insurance, on the other hand, didn't really exist until
around the 1930's. The first plans were offered by Blue Cross, which
was a group of hospitals that formed an association and basically offered
a prepaid hospital plan, followed closely by Blue Shield, which was an
association of doctors that offered a prepaid plan to cover big ticket
medical costs. Eventually, both groups merged into the Blue Cross and
Blue Shield Association.

The diversion of risk (insurance) simply means that we know there
is a risk and that the event we are insuring against is likely to happen.
We just don't know who it is going to happen to. If we take a group
of roughly 10,000 thirty-year-olds, it is pretty certain that out of that
group 9.5 will die that year, according to the National Vital Statistics
Report Vol. 54, No. 14, April 19, 2006. If each of those individuals had
$100,000 of life insurance, then the insurance company knows it will
most likely be paying out $950,000 in benefits that year. The trick, of
course, is we don't know which 9.5 people out of the 10,000 are going to
be the unlucky few. Therefore, to put this in very simplistic terms, the
insurance company has to collect $95 from each of the 10,000 members
of the group to pay the anticipated claims. To that sum, the insurance
company adds a little buffer, plus some additional to cover administrative costs and profit. All insurance is built on this concept: divide the
expected payout by the number of policyholders.

We all buy insurance because we don't know if we are about to
be one of the unlucky ones. Whether that is life insurance or health
insurance or auto insurance, we know we might be the one someday.
However, we don't see ourselves getting any benefit from it, so we hate
paying those bills. But as much as we like to believe that it "won't

happen to us," and in reality it most likely won't, we know the possibility exists. We also know there is the probability that it someday will be us (and with life insurance the probability is 100%). So maybe we can be more accepting of insurance if we think of it this way: if it is my time this year, I'm glad everyone in my "group" contributed so that my family can receive the benefit.

Since health insurance is such a hot topic as of late, it is important to understand how we got to the mess of having so many people uninsured and why 60% of all bankruptcies are caused by medical bills, as reported in a CNN Money article published June 5, 2009. Many people think that the Affordable Care Act, commonly called "Obamacare," is the problem. That is incorrect. The problem is/was the amount of medical bills that were not getting paid.

When Blue Cross and Blue Shield were first founded, they were built as non-profit entities to cover the vast majority of major medical bills. They didn't really address minor medical expenses. Then in 1973 the Health Maintenance Organization Act was passed which, in my opinion, started the slide in the wrong direction. That bill was pushed through Congress by Edgar Kaiser and President Richard Nixon. You might recognize that first name, considering the firm he founded is now one of the largest players in the health insurance field. The law said that any employer who had more than 25 employees and was offering health insurance had to offer an HMO (Health Maintenance Organization) plan as one of the options.

The idea behind HMOs was to have policyholders prepay for all of their health care, including minor visits to the doctors, with the exception of a small copay. Until that time, on average, people didn't go to the doctor for minor illnesses or injuries, such as colds, flu, splinters, etc. The HMO concept also was built on the idea of controlling more expensive visits to specialists by having people visit their general practitioner first to handle medical issues. But the concept somewhat backfired, because people felt that since they had already paid for a plan and it would only cost a small copay, they would have every minor illness or injury checked out. All of sudden, physicians were busier and could charge more money, so prices started to rise.

At the same time, greater and greater advances were occurring in the medical field, but they were not coming cheap. The "non-profit" insurance companies started seeing how much the for-profit companies were charging for their services and how much profit they were making, so they started raising their prices. Then in 1986 the Tax Reform Act caused Blue Cross and Blue Shield to lose their tax exempt status. As a result, in 1994 Blue Cross and Blue Shield allowed their licensees to become for-profit businesses, and this is when things really started to get out of control.

Now that they were full-fledged, for-profit companies, their focus changed to shareholders' profits. As a result, they began deciding who they would and would not cover and for what conditions in order to manage their risks of payouts. This led to many people being unable to buy insurance, which led to people not being able to pay their medical bills, which started the downward spiral. Since more and more people couldn't pay their bills, hospitals, clinics, and doctors began raising their prices to cover unpaid costs. I can't find a very reliable number for what percentage of medical bills go unpaid, but I found that the amount in 2011 exceeded $40 billion. And the spiral continues.

Since medical providers had to raise their fees to cover unpaid bills, the insurance companies also began to raise their rates, which led to people going without health insurance altogether or having to choose high deductible plans. However, a high deductible plan now costs so much that people cannot afford to pay the deductible when something does happen. And the end result is that providers are left with even more uncollected bills. As you can see, there was no way this could have anything but a disastrous ending.

Now you may be wondering, "Why haven't I heard these facts and figures and this history before?" Most professional writers are paid for the articles they write. In order to get paid, their article must be marketable. The people who buy their articles are publishers of papers, magazines, or information sites on the internet. And the publishers make their money by selling advertising. If their advertiser is a health care provider, what do you think the odds are that the publisher will print an article that may anger one of its advertisers if it contains information the industry doesn't want the public to know? Hence, just about everything you read in the mainstream media is going to be biased toward the product or service that is paying for the publication.

But let's turn to some insurance information and ideas that can help you keep more of your money in your own pockets.

HEALTH INSURANCE

The main components to health insurance are the premium, the copay, the deductible, the coinsurance, and a maximum out-of-pocket. Most people understand what the premium is. The copays, which are found in some policies, are what a person pays in order to obtain a service, such as you might pay $20 for a doctor visit with no further billing to you for that particular visit. The deductible is an amount of money you must pay before the insurance company starts to pay any portion of the medical bill. For example, if you have outpatient surgery and the entire bill is $4,000 but you have a $5,000 deductible, you must pay the entire amount yourself.

Coinsurance begins after you have met the deductible. If you have a 70/30 plan, it means the insurance company will start paying 70% of the bill after you have met the deductible. So let's look at a scenario where you have a $10,000 surgery bill and a $5,000 deductible with a 70/30 coinsurance plan and a $6,000 maximum out-of-pocket. In this instance, you would pay the deductible of $5,000 plus 30% of the balance until you have reached the $6,000 maximum out-of-pocket. The 30% coinsurance in this example totals $1,500, leading to your overall portion being $6,500 of the $10,000 bill, except the $6,000 maximum out-of-pocket takes effect. As a result, the insurance company would be responsible for the $500 difference.

Everybody's situation is different, but this example provides us with a glimpse into the easiest way to keep more of our money in our own pockets when it comes to health insurance. What each person has to decide, with the help of good information, is whether or not it will end up costing more or less, in the long run, to select a high deductible plan. High deductible plans cost less money, often much less money. I have seen cases where there is about a $300 premium difference per month between a $5,000 deductible and a $1,000 deductible. That means the person is paying $3,600 of their deductible every year whether they use it or not. In less than 2 years they have paid the full deductible, and if they don't use it they receive absolutely nothing for their money.

Insurance companies employ people called actuaries, who are statisticians extraordinaire. They are the ones who predict how many of each kind of illness or injury, out of a group of people, the insurance company may have to pay for in any given year. I was once invited to an insurance meeting where one of the participants was an actuary. Another attendee jokingly asked him, "How many broken elbows will there be this year?" The actuary looked him straight in the eye and asked, "Which elbow, right or left?" He then gave a specific answer and, when someone asked if he was serious, he said he was sure he was correct within a thousand. The point here is that the insurance companies know what the total risks are, so they come out the same no matter which deductible you choose. If you claim a low deductible, they are assuming more of the risk and therefore charge you more to cover their risk. The chances of you breaking your left elbow this year are exactly the same whether you choose a low deductible or a high deductible plan. The only thing that changes is the percentage of risk you are covering and the amount of risk the insurance company is covering.

Unfortunately, most people focus too much on the small risks instead looking at the long term. I know it's not any fun to pay a $5,000 medical bill, but that's not the risk our insurance protects against. The

$5,000 will hurt a little, but what we truly want to protect ourselves from are the $50,000 or $100,000 or over $200,000 bills. Try looking at it this way: let's say you have a $40,000 vehicle and the tires alone are worth $800. Would you pay $400 a year to insure the tires that you know will probably last 3 years, maybe longer? Probably not, but would you pay $200 a month to protect your total investment? Of course you would, even though you know that it won't cover the tires, or the wiper blades, or a hundred other parts.

That's how we need to look at health insurance. It insures us against loss of wealth. We are not insuring our hearts, we are insuring what it would cost to fix the heart. The average cost of a stent is about $36,000, the average cost of a hip replacement is about $39,000, and the average cost of breast cancer is around $120,000. These are the risks we are insuring against. If you have to pay one of these large bills, will you really care if your maximum out-of-pocket is $3,000 or $6,000? Odds are that someday you will have a major medical expense, but the odds are also that it won't happen too often. One of the nice things about the new health care system is that you can change your insurance every year. So if you know you have a knee replacement coming up, you can choose a low deductible, low maximum out-of-pocket plan for that year. All the other years you can pay less by buying a high deductible plan.

Try to look at it this way. The next time you are choosing a health insurance plan, stop and think, "Would I rather be the insurance company collecting the money or the policy owner paying the premium?" Chances are you would rather be the insurance company because you think they make a lot of money, and you would be correct. Remember, the insurance companies take the greatest amount of risk and yet they make money. So doesn't it make sense that if you absorb some of that risk you would also come out ahead over the long run? So the best way to stay financially intact when it comes to health insurance is to strive to buy as high a deductible as you can carry.

HSAs (Health Savings Accounts) are a great tool. An HSA is a savings account that, in many cases, can be deducted on your taxes and then used to help pay your medical bills. If you are in a 25% tax bracket and put $3,200 into an HSA account, in reality $800 of it would have been taxes paid to the government, never to be seen again. But the HSA allows you to use what would have been tax dollars to your own benefit. Not everyone qualifies for an HSA, but the idea of having a savings account just for medical purposes is still a good idea, because it allows you to comfortably afford a high deductible plan that will most likely save you money in the long run.

The last thought I'd like to share about health insurance is how the internet and the federal and state marketplaces are creating a false sense of security. Advertisements advise you to sign up for coverage either by going online or calling the marketplaces, but what is not addressed is how to select the right coverage for you. You can find experts to help you navigate the websites, but the vast majority of them are not licensed insurance agents, so they can't explain the benefits or the differences among various plans. The policy will cost you the exact same price whether you use a licensed professional agent or not, so why wouldn't you avail yourself of their expertise? You absolutely should not make your decision by what you read or hear through the commercials.

LIFE INSURANCE

Why do they call it life insurance? After all, it doesn't guarantee that you will keep on living. I think life insurance should be called "survivor's security insurance," since its true purpose is to allow you to leave money behind to pay off bills and help your survivors attain the dreams you wanted to provide for them. Life insurance is the only totally self-fulfilling financial planning tool as long as you hold it until the plan is fulfilled or the insurance fulfills it for you.

Let's say you are a young parent and you want to make sure your family always has a roof over its head, food on the table, and the kids attend college if they so choose. If you live to a ripe old age and plan right, you will be able to see all those plans come to pass. If, on the other hand, you die unexpectedly after having paid only a few premiums on a life insurance policy, the insurance will make it possible for your spouse or partner to ensure that all the plans you made together still come true.

However, there are several big problems that occur when purchasing life insurance. Many people buy too much, others buy too little, some pay way too much, and some just buy the wrong type at the wrong time. Most of what the general public learns about life insurance is taught to them by insurance salespeople. So depending on the bias of the salesperson, the education will be tainted in a certain direction and to a certain set of beliefs. So let's first cover the different types of life insurance.

TERM INSURANCE

Term insurance is used to meet a large need for insurance for a specified period of time, such as to pay off a mortgage or to provide income for a family until the children are grown. It is simple and straightforward. The amount of the insurance usually remains the same for the entire period of time selected and so does the premium. When it comes up for renewal it will be priced at your current age, so it is best to buy for the longest period that you can afford and not let the coverage lapse.

People both love and hate term insurance. They love it because it is cheap to buy, but as people get close to the end of the term, many resent not having received anything for the premiums they paid over all those years. It's best to remember that with term insurance we are essentially renting the coverage for the specified time period. When you rent a car and you return it in the same condition (except for added mileage), you don't expect the rental company to refund your money, because you know you had the use of that vehicle and, hopefully, you feel that you received your money's worth.

You should feel the same way about term life insurance. We don't know if we are going to be one of the unlucky few or one of the lucky many. However, we can be assured that if we do become one of the unlucky few, the insurance will be worth many times what we paid for it.

We rented the coverage because, just like with renting a car, it is cheaper than buying one and then trying to sell it back to someone a week later.

One of the big problems with term insurance is that people often keep the wrong amount for too long. With life insurance, especially term, we are betting that we are going to die early, and the insurance company is basically betting that we will not. So, once again, would you rather be the insurance company or the policy owner? The problem comes when someone has paid premiums on a $500,000 policy for the last 20 years. But after 20 years the kids are grown, the home mortgage hopefully has been reduced, and that need for full coverage no longer exists. Unfortunately, the policy owner gets stuck on the idea that unless they keep the coverage at $500,000 they will never get their money's worth. But they did. They bought 20 years of peace of mind, and that is exactly what they received.

So now the policyholder needs to look at the next purchase on its own merits. The past is the past, and the money spent is no different than the money you spend on any other purchase. Once a product is used up, you decide if you want to purchase a new product, one that fits your new set of needs. When we are younger and raising children we need bigger cars and bigger houses. As we grow older and the kids move out, we tend to gravitate to smaller vehicles and homes. Insurance should be viewed the same way.

UNIVERSAL LIFE

Universal Life is a cross between whole life and term life. Inside the policy, the insurance buys term insurance on a yearly basis. You pay a lot more than you would for term insurance in the beginning but less than you would at the end. The extra money you put into the policy at the beginning will accumulate to help you pay the higher premiums at the end. Universal life policies are good for those who can afford them, because it is like building your own bank. In later years you can borrow from the cash value of the policy for any purpose that you choose. Of course, if you don't pay the loan back, your policy will eventually run out of cash and you will lose your coverage.

These policies especially make sense for people in their 50's or 60's. The reason is that you can only buy term insurance until the age of 80, so if you plan to live longer than that and have insurance, you would probably want to consider a universal life policy. Many of the old policies were structured extremely poorly, in that many times they did not build enough cash to keep the policy in force past the age of 80, and when policyholders reached that age it became so expensive to keep the policy in force they ended up losing all their coverage. However, there is a much better version of universal life offered these days, which guarantees that the policy will stay in force until age 121 as long as you keep paying the predetermined premium. If you are considering buying a universal life policy, you need to be looking at this version. With a universal life policy, we are no longer buying for the "just in case" scenario, we are buying for the "we know the time is coming" scenario.

SINGLE PREMIUM WHOLE LIFE

Single Premium is a great tool for attaining a couple of goals. It is a way to instantly increase your estate for your loved ones and control your income taxes at the same time. It is also the most efficient way to buy insurance and to make sure that you don't pay more for the insurance than what you will collect someday. With single premium insurance, you pay a set amount of money once, the insurance company determines how much insurance coverage that will buy for you, and then you never pay again and the insurance stays in effect until the day you need it. The policy will usually grow in both cash value and death benefit over time. However, since all the administrative costs occur when the policy is issued, many times it will take several years before your cash value starts to grow.

With all that said, there are a few companies offering policies where the cash value is never less than what you put into the contract and the death benefit starts growing from the very first year. These products can be especially good for people who have one of the older, or more poorly written, universal life products. In that circumstance, it can make more sense to cash out when the cash value is near its highest point and use that cash to purchase a fully paid, single premium policy. If there is any way you can afford it, these policies are also a much better alternative to the final expense policies that we discuss next.

FINAL EXPENSE POLICIES

Final Expense policies, also known as Burial, are whole life insurance products, meaning that you will pay on these until you die or reach age 100, whichever comes first. They are typically smaller life insurance policies written for amounts from $2,000 to $25,000. Many people have some life insurance, and many times these are small, fully paid policies that were purchased many years ago. However, what $5,000 bought 20 or 30 years ago is nowhere near what it will buy today. In these instances, people need to buy just a little more insurance to make sure that all their final expenses can be paid with insurance proceeds.

However, the way in which these policies are generally marketed is where the problem lies. In television and direct mail advertisements, companies will claim they offer guaranteed coverage. But once you look at the fine print in the policy, you find you are only guaranteed for the first 2 or 3 years to get back the money you paid in. It isn't until after the third year that you will actually get more than you paid in. Once you do the math though, you will also discover that you will have paid in enough money over the first 9 years to cover the entire death benefit, yet to keep the insurance in force you must keep paying the premiums. Thus, many people end up paying in more than their families will ever collect.

As an example, let's say you are paying about $100 per month for a $10,000 policy, which is not uncommon. By the end of the 9th year you will have paid in $10,800, but you only have a cash value of $7,000 to $8,000. So what do you do? Do you keep paying the premium so that someday your family gets the whole $10,000 or do you consider yourself lucky to have survived and simply take the cash and set it aside and cut your losses? I highly recommend if you are young enough and can qualify, put the money into one of the single premium life policies that were previously discussed.

OTHER LIFE INSURANCE

Just a couple more quick thoughts about a few other kinds of life insurance. One that is still around, and unfortunately mostly sold to the people who can least afford to make a mistake, is mortgage life insurance, which is built specifically to pay off a mortgage. As the mortgage balance is reduced, so too does the amount of life insurance. Even that by itself does not make it a bad product, but the problem is the price people pay for this product. Insurance companies sell it in what is called a simplified form and they usually don't do much underwriting, which allows them to sell it quickly and deliver it quickly before the policyholders find out that they probably could have bought better coverage for the same price. It is more of an emotional sale then a logical sale. If you are ever considering mortgage life insurance, please take the time to look at a regular term life policy. Chances are you can get more for your money.

Then there is the ever famous "accidental death" benefit. It shouldn't be hard for anyone to see that these are just huge money-makers for the insurance companies. For example, if it costs $30 per month for the first $250,000 of insurance coverage, yet you can add the accidental death benefit for another $250,000 for less than $10 per month, that should be an indication, especially when the number one cause of death for young people is accidents. If you're buying insurance because you need the coverage, then simply buy $500,000 of coverage in the first place.

LONG TERM CARE INSURANCE

Long term care, also known as nursing home insurance, is once again something I don't typically recommend purchasing. It's not that I don't believe in the concept, but after more than 30 years in this business, I think I have known only two people who actually collected a benefit from this type of insurance. To collect on a long term care policy, you must be unable to perform at least two out of six specific "activities of daily living:" bathing, dressing, feeding oneself, mobility (the ability to walk across a room and get up from a bed or chair), personal hygiene (brushing hair and teeth), and toileting. A female client of mine needed assistance with bathing and putting on socks and shoes, yet this was not counted by the insurance company because she could still button a shirt or blouse and put on slacks. Another client could get out of a chair and walk but needed help getting out of bed. The insurance company decided she was mobile "enough" and denied her claim.

I also have a problem with the statistics the companies use to sell their products. One claims that when you consider everyone over the age of 65, 50% of the people will eventually require some skilled nursing care. Although that number is true, what they don't reveal is the large percentage of stays that will not qualify for benefits under the most common terms for these kinds of policies. Many stays only last a few weeks, such as when recovering from surgery or major illness. Most long term care policies have what is called an elimination period of typically 3 or 6 months in order to keep the premiums affordable. If you remove all the short stays that long term care insurance will not pay for, the percentage of people over 65 who will actually qualify for a long term care benefit drops between 5% and 20%. Just because you are in a nursing home does not mean you are going to qualify for a nursing home benefit. Long term care policies are expensive, and on average you don't see a return on your money if you never qualify to use the benefit.

As an alternative, there are a few companies that sell a life insurance contract that can double as a long term care benefit. This kind of policy will usually pay 2% of the face amount of the policy as a long term care benefit. Thus, if you have a $100,000 policy, it will pay $2,000 a month as a long term care benefit. And an added benefit of these policies is that someone in the family eventually will inherit the remaining value in the event of your death. For example, if you used $50,000 of the $100,000 face value as a long term care benefit during your lifetime, upon your death your heirs would get the remaining $50,000. This is a much more logical and efficient way of using your money to meet your needs, without wasting it.

When examining alternatives, it is important to understand the reasons why a person wants to buy long term care insurance. Most people will say they don't want Medicaid to take away their house and all their assets. But deep down the actual reason is that they don't want to use up all the assets on their own welfare so that they can leave something for their heirs. If that, indeed, is the real objective, life insurance is a better way to accomplish the goal. However, clients will argue that Medicaid can still take the cash value or death benefit of life insurance as an asset. That's true, so the trick is to have someone else own the insurance policy. There is an easy way and a little bit more complicated way to accomplish this task.

The easy method is to gift the money to your most responsible heir to buy the policy and make the payments. You can do this because the government allows any one person to give another individual up to $14,000 per year without any tax consequences to either party. The more complicated method involves getting legal help to draw up an Irrevocable Life Insurance Trust (ILIT). Once again, the "insured" person gives the money up-front to the beneficiaries and the beneficiaries then pay the premiums. When the person passes away, the trust gets the proceeds and distributes them to the beneficiaries per the terms of the trust. Oftentimes this method is used so that several years of premiums can be placed in the trust in advance. This allows your heirs sufficient money to pay future premiums while allowing you to retain your Medicaid eligibility, whereas making a gift would count against you financially. Be aware, though, that to pursue an ILIT you will need a good life insurance policy that will stay in effect until the end of your life and a competent lawyer to fully explain all the rules and to draw up the trust document.

FINAL THOUGHTS

To stay financially intact, we need to walk that fine line between not being covered at all and becoming insurance poor. All insurance decisions are very tightly tied to emotional events, so the best advice is to make your decisions from a logical point of view. Examine what you are truly trying to accomplish and whether the options make sense from today forward. We should learn from the past, but what we have done in the past does not necessarily fit our current goals.

Chapter 6

MONEY

"Wealth is the ability to fully experience life"

HENRY DAVID THOREAU

The first premise of this book is, "Making money is easy, keeping it is the hard part." While to this point we have focused on all the ways people try to part you from your money, we will now discuss how "making money is easy." There are many ways to make money. We can work for it, we can invest wisely, or we can own a business. To invest well, we can put our money in a bank, we can purchase real estate, we can invest in the stock market or annuities or market linked CDs and a host of other products. We won't cover all the ways of making money in this chapter, because there are already many financial planning books that cover the subject. Instead, in this chapter we will focus on the myths that have been generally accepted as true that prevent you from earning more than you could be. We will also discuss a couple of opportunities that are either overlooked or ignored because of misunderstandings.

I teach a class called the C.A.S.H. system. C stands for cash, A for annuities, S for the stock market, and H for housing (real estate). I am a believer in true diversification. A lot of advisors and salespersons mouth these words, but then it doesn't remain a focus when it comes to investing in their particular product. I think insurance agents and stockbrokers are the worst when it comes to this. Stockbrokers think diversification means owning 20 different mutual funds, and insurance agents think life insurance and annuities makes you diversified. My advice is that you need some money in each of the four major asset classes: cash, annuities, stock market, and real estate. So let's start with the basics. Every product or class of products has strong points and weak points.

As you can see from the chart, you always have to give up something to get something. Just like we have been told all our lives, "there is no free ride." Everything in life has a price. To earn more you have to give up either time (liquidity) or take more risk. It depends on the level of safety or growth you desire as to how much liquidity and growth you are willing to trade to achieve your desired result.

C	A	S	H
Banks	Fixed Annuities	Stocks	Housing
Money Markets	I Bonds	Bonds	Real Estate
Savings	Market Linked CDs	Mutual Funds	
CDs		ETFs	
Very Liquid	Partially Liquid	Very Liquid	Not Liquid
Only goes up in value	Only goes up in value	Value fluctuates up or down	Value usually goes up
Not much growth	Moderate growth	Growth or loss	Moderate growth

C - CASH PRODUCTS

As we see from the chart, cash products are very liquid and very safe, but the problem is you can't really make any money with them, especially in the last few years. This brings forth a new way of losing. Although we can't lose principal with cash, we can lose purchasing power if we are not making enough to keep up with inflation.

We all need some of our wealth in the cash classification. We need it to cover emergencies and to have available when new opportunities arise. Only you know what is the correct percentage or amount to have in this category. Everyone has different needs, wants, and comfort levels. In my opinion, you should have no less than 6 months of total income in this category and, unless you have a special need coming up in the near term, probably no more than a full 2 years' income. If we don't have enough money in this category, we could end up paying a penalty to bring in money from one of the other categories, but if we have too much we could lose our battle with inflation.

Here are a couple of ideas to help you manage your cash. As far as money markets are concerned, shop around. Sometimes brokerage firms pay a higher amount than banks do. Also, I have seen at times where some of the charge card companies pay a fair amount of interest if you place your savings with them. So keep your options and your eyes open for opportunities.

Certificates of deposit (CDs) can be purchased through a method called laddering. Take the total amount that you plan to put into CDs and then buy 4 separate CDs. Buy one 6-month CD, one 12-month, one 18-month, and one 2-year CD. As each CD matures you simply renew it as a 2-year CD. When the first one comes due, you only have 6 months left on the 1-year CD and 18 months on the 2-year CD, so that is why you then keep buying 2-year CDs. (Of course, you can vary this method by buying 1-year, 2-year, 3-year and 4-year CDs instead.)

The reason to ladder is two-fold. First, it helps with liquidity, but more importantly, especially in years with really low interest rates, you consistently have money coming due. So once rates start to rise, and they will, you will be able to move your money consistently into products with higher paying interest rates in a fairly short period of time. You won't have a lot of your money stuck for a long period of time in a low interest CD. And then once we return to reasonable interest rates, you start a new ladder with longer time frames, so that you can keep as much of your money working at the higher interest rates. Interest rates are at historical lows, but the average since 1950 is above 4%. We will see higher interest rates again someday. The Wall Street chapter has a further discussion about why current interest rates are low when the stock market is at all-time highs.

A – ANNUITIES

Annuities are, or at least can be, tax deferred products. From the CASH chart you will see that they are safe, because the values can only go up, not down. It must be pointed out that I am talking about fixed and fixed indexed annuities here, not variable annuities. What we give up for this safety is that we can make more money in products that assume more risk. On the other hand, what we give up to earn more than the bank products is part of our liquidity.

Annuities were invented by the Romans thousands of years ago. The Romans needed money to finance their campaign to conquer and control the rest of the world, so they came up with the concept of an "annua." If you loaned your money to the government, they would provide you with an income for the rest of your life. The start of modern day tax deferred annuities came into existence in the United States in 1912, just one year before income taxes were established. They were likely the first of many tax loopholes to come. Since then, annuities have evolved into a more flexible, useful investment tool. They do not always have a good reputation, but you need to consider the source. Since Wall Street can't offer the guarantees of principal and lifetime income like an annuity can, and banks can only offer lower returns because of their high overhead, you can understand why they view annuities as competition rather than a part of a sound financial portfolio.

An annuity is a type of savings account that is issued by an insurance company rather than a bank. They are not FDIC insured, but they do have strong guarantees behind them. For one, they have the claims-paying ability of the insurance company as a strength. Because insurance companies are regulated by the states rather than the federal government, state laws mandate that insurance companies maintain what are called "reserves." The reserves mean that the insurance companies have enough liquid assets available to pay off all potential liabilities. Furthermore, all states now have what are called "state guarantor laws" or acts. These acts give states the right to charge a premium to every insurance company that does business in the state in order to cover any losses that might be incurred should any of the companies become insolvent.

In other words, if one company does go into reorganization, all the other companies have to chip in and make good on the policy guarantees provided to clients. No one can lose money in an annuity so long as they stay within the boundaries of the guarantees. The guarantees usually provide for $100,000 per person. The nice thing about these guarantees is that, unlike FDIC insured bank accounts, not only is your principal guaranteed but so is at least a minimum amount of interest.

The minimum interest guarantee varies greatly from company to company and from product to product, but it is usually somewhere between 1% and 3%. There are two other great benefits to annuities. One allows you to withdraw funds from the annuity without paying early withdrawal charges, which you would find with CDs and some mutual funds. With almost all annuities, you are able to withdraw 10% of your balance with no penalty. Let's say, for example, that you put $50,000 in a CD and $50,000 in an annuity and then an emergency came up and you needed to withdraw $5,000. With the CD, you would be charged an early withdrawal penalty, on average, of 6 months' interest based on the entire amount. In this example, the penalty would add up to $3,000. Alternatively, you would be able to withdraw $5,000 from the annuity with zero penalty.

Let's take that one step further and say you needed to withdraw $10,000 instead. With the CD you would have the same result: a

$3,000 penalty. With the annuity you may have to pay as much as a 10% penalty, but only on the amount over and above the free 10% withdrawal amount. In this example, that would add up to $500 (10% of $5,000), which is still substantially better than the $3,000 penalty on the CD.

The greatest benefit of annuities, though, is the fact that they grow tax deferred. This means there are no taxes paid on the earnings until you withdraw the earnings. You get to control when you pay the taxes on those earnings. This also gives you the power, in many instances, to control when and if you will pay taxes on other income, such as Social Security income or IRA withdrawals. When set up correctly by a good tax advisor, annuities can even be used to help people move money out of their IRAs absolutely tax free.

There are 4 types of annuities: immediate, fixed, variable, and fixed indexed.

IMMEDIATE ANNUITIES

Immediate annuities are exactly what they say they are. You take a certain amount of money and give it to an insurance company, and in return they give you guaranteed monthly income checks for life. There are slight variations, such as you can choose a predetermined amount of years instead of a lifetime income, but the most common form is for lifetime, just like the original concept put forth and practiced by Roman society. This is the product that was used by most pension plans, when there were still companies that had pension plans. The companies would accumulate funds for the pension while the person was working, but at the end they would use the funds to purchase for their pensioner a guaranteed lifetime income from an insurance company. For example, I know a woman who retired from Montgomery Ward a few years before it went bankrupt. Montgomery Ward closed its doors in 2000, but to this day she gets her monthly checks from the insurance company that was used to buy her pension.

The amount of the payment is determined by two factors: the prevailing interest rate and the age of the person. So if you are going to use an annuity to build your own pension, and you believe that interest rates are going to rise in the next year, you might try to wait for a year. You will get a higher monthly income for the rest of your life because you are both a year older (unfortunately that also means one less year of life expectancy) and the rate per thousand could rise because of higher interest rates.

FIXED ANNUITIES

Fixed annuities are a very simple product. They most closely resemble certificates of deposits, in that you invest an amount of money with the insurance company for a fixed time period and in return you will receive a fixed interest rate for that period. In a couple of ways they are better and in a couple of ways they are not. CDs can be bought for short periods of time, from 3-month to 5-year time periods, while fixed annuities can be bought for 5-year to 10-year time periods. CDs can be cashed in a matter of a few minutes. Annuities pay a little more interest for two reasons. One is that insurance companies don't have the high overhead that banks do. The second reason is that you normally are committing to a longer period of time. Annuities grow tax deferred, whereas with CDs you generally pay taxes on the interest as it is earned. Lastly, with annuities you have some access to your principal on a yearly basis, whereas with CDs you do not. This makes it a little easier to commit your money for a longer period of time. If you do decide to invest in an annuity, you can use the same laddering technique that I outlined in the section on CDs. In this instance, you might buy a 5-year, a 7-year, and a 10-year annuity.

VARIABLE ANNUITIES

Variable annuities have some of the attributes of the other annuities, but they do not have the same guarantees as the other forms do. Variable annuities are basically mutual funds wrapped around an annuity shell so that it obtains tax deferred status. Most insurance companies call the funds inside their annuities "investment options," but the government sites always call the options mutual funds, which is what they truly are. They do not and cannot actually guarantee your principal because of how the funds are invested. However, the company will try to tell you that your money is guaranteed, and in a way it is, but you need to understand how the guarantee works. In this case, and only in this case, when it comes to annuities the guarantee only exists if you are willing to take the money that no longer really exists over a period of time. They usually refer to what is called a high water mark. Let's say you invest $100,000 and it eventually grows to $130,000 and then drops back down to $120,000. The company's guarantee says that you will get the $130,000, but the fine print says you can withdraw approximately $119,000 in cash and get the balance in periodic payments over a period of time, such as 5 or 10 years.

The other guarantee insurance companies like to tout is one that guarantees you "7% for as long as you live." Notice the wording. You have to pay attention to the details. They did not guarantee a 7% return on your money. Instead, they will give you 7% of the value of the account on the day you elect this option. If your account balance is $100,000, they are guaranteeing they will pay you $7,000 per year as long as you live. But here's how it is an empty guarantee.

If you earned no further interest on that $100,000 balance, it would take a little over 14 years for the account to run out of money. But consider that most people don't start something like this until their late 60's or early 70's. And when you turn on this option, some of the companies immediately take the money out of the market and put it into a fixed interest rate account, while others let you keep it invested in the market.

For this example, let's assume that the $100,000 will average 3% earnings rate during the time period that you are withdrawing the 7%. Under those circumstances, it would take 18 years for the account to run out of money. But to top that off, you have to pay an extra fee to obtain this "guarantee," which is used to buy insurance on that money. If you do outlive the 14- or 18-year payout, the insurance kicks in and pays the benefit so that the insurance company won't lose money. In the end you actually bought your "guarantee." So the bottom line is, you can lose money with variable annuities.

The other two things I don't like about variable annuities is (1) they are expensive and (2), although you are invested in the stock market, with all its risk, when you withdraw your money you lose your capital gains tax rate advantage. All money that comes out of an annuity is taxed as interest at the higher regular income tax rates. The final weakness is that your heirs also don't receive "step up in basis" with annuities the way they would with regular stocks or mutual funds. They lose the "step up in basis" because of the tax deferred growth that you received over the years. So when I look at all the things you give up, the lack of true guarantees of principal, and the fees involved, I believe you would be better off using other products.

This brings us back to the C.A.S.H. system. You need money in each of the areas, because they all have their strengths and weaknesses. We should not be trying to build one product that encompasses all the good parts and thinking that we can work around the weaknesses. It can't be done, because every product has its weaknesses. There is no combination that will eliminate all the weaknesses without creating new ones.

INDEXED ANNUITIES

I'm going to take some time to explain indexed annuities to you for 3 reasons:

1. There are a lot of parts and pieces to this investment alternative that need to be understood.
2. Although a good alternative, many people are not buying indexed annuities because the salesperson either cannot or does not take the time to explain them thoroughly and, as a result, the buyer doesn't trust either the product or the salesperson.
3. On the other hand, some people buy them but then are dissatisfied because the salesperson sold them incorrectly, leaving the buyer having expected one result but received another.

Indexed annuities are a unique product that allow the owners to participate in the gains of the stock market but not in the down trends of the market. When the market goes up, an indexed annuity credits a portion of that upward move to the owner in the form of an interest payment, but when the market goes down the annuity will hold its last "locked in" value. Earnings in an indexed annuity are considered interest because it is a guaranteed principal product.

Indexed annuities came into existence in 1995. They are considered a fixed annuity because they guarantee that you cannot lose money. In most cases, they actually guarantee that you will make at least a little interest. Indexed annuities also guarantee that once earnings are credited to the account you can never again lose that money. It is that last part of the guarantee that makes these contracts so unique and valuable. It is also the part that helps the returns on these contracts keep pace, or even at times outperform, other popular investments.

"TOO GOOD TO BE TRUE?"

If you are like me, you are probably thinking right now that this sounds too good to be true and therefore it is probably just that. However, if you will read through this section you will come to understand the mechanics of this investment product and understand how indexed annuities can and do work exactly as described.

Let's say you invest $100,000 into a fixed indexed annuity. Let's further say the insurance company guarantees that, at a minimum, they will pay you 1% interest on 90% of your deposit over the next 10 years. (Over the years, this guarantee has ranged from 1% on 87% of the money deposited to 3% on 100% of the money, depending on the prevailing interest rates at the time.) At the 1% on 90% formula, it means they guarantee that, at the worst, they will cash out your policy at the end of 10 years for $110,462. Now let's assume that the insurance company is actually earning 5% on the money they manage. Insurance companies operate on about a 2% margin to pay all their bills. This is much lower than banks, because they only have a fraction of the number of employees or buildings, hence their overhead is much lower. So if the company is making 5%, that means it is actually earning an extra 3% that they could be paying you. Their commitment to you is the 1% minimum return at the end of the contract. This is what frees up the money to make the indexed portion of this investment work.

To honor the guarantee in this example, the company only needs to invest about $82,000 at the 3%. Therefore, the insurance company now has about $18,000 to buy options on the S&P 500. This is how an indexed annuity helps you to participate in the movement in the market without being invested in the market. The annuity doesn't buy the S&P 500, only the options. An option is the right to buy something at a given price at a given time.

I'm going to briefly digress here because it is important to understand how options work, and thus understand how an indexed annuity works. An option gives the buyer the right to buy, but not the obligation. An option seller has the obligation to sell it at the stated price at the stated time, but if the buyer chooses not to buy then the seller retains the option money and the asset.

For example, let's say you wanted to sell your house and it is worth $250,000. Someone from out of state says they would like to buy your house for cash, but because they aren't retiring until the next year they want to buy your house at full price one year from now. While you are contemplating the offer, you consider that prices might go up over the year and so you would be giving up potential profit. However, after recent history, you are thinking it could also go down in value, and if you don't make this deal you might end up selling for less. So you tell the potential buyer that you are willing to make that deal if the buyer will give you $5,000 right now and you get to keep the money whether or not he actually buys the house one year from now.

If the buyer agrees, you have just sold the option and the buyer has purchased the option. A year goes by and houses like yours are now selling for $265,000, so the buyer exercises his option and buys your house for the $250,000 and finds himself $10,000 ahead. On the other hand, if houses like yours are worth only $235,000 one year later, the buyer will not exercise his option to buy your house. Although he lost the initial $5,000 investment, it is better than losing the $15,000.

So now back to our previous example. The insurance company takes the $18,000 it has to invest, breaks it into 10 parts so it has money to buy the options every year for the next 10 years, and then it purchases those options. If the market is up for the year, they exercise the option and you make the money. If the market is down, that year's option money is gone but everything else stays intact. The $82,000 principal remains safe and earning its 3%, and the subsequent years' option money is intact so that the whole process can begin again the following year. However, especially in this low interest rate market, this is exactly why indexed annuities do not get the full movement of the market. There isn't enough money in the original $100,000 investment to buy enough options to cover the entire movement of the market, therefore limits have to be set as to how much you can actually make in any given year.

The following chart shows what an indexed annuity might look like versus how the market is actually performing. These numbers are completely fictional; I am simply showing you the concept in numerical form.

As you can see, even though you are only getting 60% of the upside, you can do pretty well with this concept. There are many methods the insurance companies have to determine how they will calculate the amount of interest that will be paid to you. It's the "many methods" that make indexed annuities difficult to understand, although the concept is generally quite simple. If the market goes up you make money, if the market goes down you stay right where you were. You don't make anything but you don't lose anything. Among the "many methods" for crediting interest to you, there are three basic ones along with three ways that limit the amount each of the methods can produce as a final result.

Sample $10,000 account

year	Percentage gain/loss	S&P 500 Mutual Fund	Indexed Annuity 60% participation No Cap
Start		10,000	10000
1	10%	11,000	10600
2	15%	12,650	11,554
3	-8%	11,638	11,554
4	-12%	10,241	11,554
5	20%	12,290	12,940

The limitations are called participation rates, caps, and margins (sometimes called "spreads").

Participation rates are exactly as they sound. They may be listed as something like 60% or 50% or 35%. If your annuity has a 60% participation rate and the method you chose would produce a 10% return in its entirety, then the interest that will be credited to your annuity account for that time period will be 6% (60% of 10%). You will understand this better once we show how it works with the methods.

Caps are the second form of limitation and this one is also, by itself, easy to understand. We have seen caps over the years in the low teens, but with today's low interest rates, caps are much more likely to be in the 3% to 6% range. So again assuming the method you chose would pay in its entirety a 10% return and your cap was 5%, then your annuity account would be credited with 5% for the year. On the other hand, if the method produced a 4% return (under the 5% cap), you would receive the entire 4%.

The third method isn't seen as much today but it is still around and quite effective at times. It is called the margin or the spread. Many times this method is used more in current years along with a participation rate. If the two were not combined, it would mean that if you had a margin of 3% then you would get everything over the 3% up to whatever the market produced. Thus, if the market produced 10% you would get 7%, if the market gained 20% you would get 17%. These are usually called fees within the contracts, because the governing agencies demand that they be called that. A fee, when looked at with any other investment product, gets charged whether or not the account makes money. Since indexed annuities can't lose money, these fees cannot be charged unless the contract makes at least that much money. Therefore, the term is called a margin or a spread and should be understood to be exactly that.

As stated earlier there are 3 major interest crediting methods from among 40 or so varieties, but you can reduce all of them down to the 3 basic methods. They are the monthly averaging method, the monthly sum method, and the point to point method.

The point to point method was the original method of indexed annuities and basically is the most efficient. It doesn't always produce the best results, but it is the most efficient. In the early versions the point to point could be as long as a 10-year period. The first "point" is the day the original investment is tied to the performance of the market. The second "point" is where the market ends up at the conclusion of the time period. I am going to show you examples of each method using the opening price of the S&P 500 index on Jan. 2, 2014 and the closing price of the S&P 500 on Dec. 31, 2014.

The point to point has evolved now to basically a yearly time frame, although a few remaining companies continue to use a two-year period. So in this example, the opening price on Jan. 2, 2014 was $1845.86, and the closing number for year on Dec. 31, 2014 was $2058.20. In the point to point method, we subtract the first number from the last number and end up with a difference of $212.34. So if you invested straight into the market and then sold at the end of the year you would have made 11.5% on your investment. If you were invested in an indexed annuity with a cap rate of 5.5%, you would have made 5.5%. If, instead, the point to point was calculated on a participation rate basis of 35%, you would have made 4.02% (35% of 11.5%). You will see in the chapter on Wall Street that if you take all the "up" years since 1950 and averaged them out, the average is approximately 13%. So using that figure as our basis and taking our best guess that the average will stay in that range, the correct choice to make between a participation rate and a cap is figured like this. We take 13% and then multiply that by the offered participation rate. If the result is larger than the cap, we would select the participation rate, but if not larger we would select the cap. As an example, if the participation rate is 50%, the cap would have to be higher than 6.5% to make it worthwhile to take the cap.

Monthly averaging is the second crediting method. The formula is quite simple. You again take the starting number of the S&P 500 but this time you find the ending number for each of the next 12 months. At the end of the year you add up the 12 monthly ending numbers and then divide that sum by 12. You then subtract that number from the beginning number, take that figure and divide it by the beginning number, and you have your percentage that your contract will earn for the year, limited by the cap or other limiting function. In this instance, the cap is almost always used. The chart below shows you how a contract would have performed using the 2014 numbers.

Monthly Averaging		
Jan. 2 2014	Beginning Number	
	1845.86	
end		
Jan. 31	1782.59	
Feb. 28	1859.45	
Mar. 31	1872.34	
April. 30	1883.95	
May. 30	1923.57	
June. 30	1960.23	
July. 31	1930.67	
Aug. 29	2003.37	
Sept. 30	1972.29	
Oct. 31	2018.05	
Nov. 28	2067.56	
Dec. 31	2058.9	
Total	23332.97	
Divided by 12	1944.41	Average for the year
subtract starting number	-1845.86	
Gain for year	98.55	

Divide that number by the beginning number and you get the percentage gain (interest) credited to the account for the year. 5.3%

Monthly sum is the third of the crediting methods. This one uses a cap but on a monthly basis instead of a yearly basis. In this method we take the beginning number of the index at the beginning of each month and then we take the ending number for each month. We subtract one from the other, divide the answer by the beginning number, and that is the percentage we apply to that month for the computation. This method almost always uses a cap. The two important things to remember are that the cap is only for the upside, there is no cap on the downside. The second thing is that it is a monthly cap, which means the most amount earned could be a very large number. For example, if the monthly cap is 2%, then in theory the account could earn 24% in one year. However this is unlikely, simply because the market never goes up by 2% or more for 12 months in a row. During quickly rising markets, this is an excellent choice. The trick is, of course, we never know in advance when we are going to have a really good, fast-moving market. Once again I am using in the following chart the numbers from 2014.

Monthly Sum			
Jan. 2 2014	Beginning Number 1845.86	Percentage Change per month	Cap Limit
end			
Jan. 31	1782.59	-3.42%	-3.42%
Feb. 28	1859.45	4.31%	2.00%
Mar. 31	1872.34	0.69%	0.69%
April. 30	1883.95	0.62%	0.62%
May. 30	1923.57	2.10%	2.00%
June. 30	1960.23	1.90%	1.90%
July. 31	1930.67	-1.50%	-1.50%
Aug. 29	2003.37	3.76%	2.00%
Sept. 30	1972.29	-1.55%	-1.55%
Oct. 31	2018.05	2.32%	2.00%
Nov. 28	2067.56	2.45%	2.00%
Dec. 31	2058.9	-0.42%	0.42%
			7.16% Amount of interest credited for the year.

Each method works and each method works best during certain types of markets. The trouble is that none of us knows what the market is going to do over the next 12 months. So the way we use these methods is to place a portion of the annuity contract into each one of the methods, basically on an even split. There has been a new feature added, the Lifetime Benefit Income Rider (LIBR), that in some ways makes these products work better when using them to build yourself a pension. Unfortunately when interest rates dropped to historical lows, salespeople started selling this new feature because it sounded good. What these riders state is that they guarantee you that the lifetime income benefit will grow by 7% per year. Unfortunately, too many salespeople sell this as a guaranteed 7% growth rate without putting the emphasis on the fact that it only applies to the lifetime benefit.

The annuity account is tracked in two different ways: the cash account and the income benefit account. In the cash account, the money grows according to whatever method you chose, along with its limitations. The income account, which can only be used for deducing what the income is going to be, grows by the guaranteed income account percentage rate. The number from the income account can never be cashed out; it is only used to determine how much income will be generated. The cash account is charged a fee for the life of the contract to have this extra feature, and the guaranteed rate only lasts for a specified number of years or until the benefit starts to pay out a monthly income. All of this is okay so long as your main purpose is to create a pension, a lifetime income that cannot be outlived. When, on the other hand, it is not a certainty that the money will be used for pension purposes, then it is an incorrect choice.

Indexed annuities are a good alternative investment to such things as CDs and bonds. They are 100% safe, partially liquid, and offer a reasonable rate of return. Like every other investment product, when used correctly indexed annuities have a place in most people's portfolios for a portion of their money. As people get closer to retirement or are in retirement, they become more focused on protecting their money.

Therefore, the safety factor plus the reasonable rate of return offered by indexed annuities make them a good choice.

MARKET LINKED CD'S

Like every other certificate of deposit, market linked CDs are FDIC insured. They are a good product for those who wish to have an opportunity to achieve a high rate of return while keeping their money safe. Of course, as with every other financial product, if you are going to get something more in one area, you have to give up something in the benefits. In the case of market linked CDs, you give up liquidity, agree to a longer term contract, and make a higher minimum investment to purchase one, compared to other choices. This type of CD used to be sold primarily to the very wealthy because the minimums were extremely high, but in recent years a few firms have found a way to allow more people to participate by lowering the minimum contracts to approximately $20,000. When you first look at these CDs they look quite appealing, but when you examine the specifics they seem to lose a bit of their luster.

I BONDS

I bonds are an interesting investment alternative that are very seldom discussed. They can be an excellent choice for money that you wish to set aside for some time in the future yet keep your principal safe. They will become a better investment once interest rates start to rise again. The I bond is issued by the U.S. government and pays two interest rates. One is a basic rate that is set at the time you purchase the bond and the other is a floating rate. The interest is paid the first of every month and is compounded semi-annually. The floating rate (the government calls it a variable semi-annual inflation rate) is based on the change in the Consumer Price Index for all Urban Consumers (CPI-U). The Bureau of the Fiscal Service announces the rates each May and November. The semi-annual inflation rate announced in May represents the change between the CPI-U figures from the preceding September and March; the inflation rate announced in November is the change between the CPI-U figures from the preceding March and September.

The interest is paid within the bond, not in cash, and therefore it is tax deferred. You don't pay taxes on the interest until you cash in the bond. We talked earlier about the power of tax deferral and its many uses, so I am sure you are aware of how strong a feature this is. I bonds are a long term investment and should only be purchased when you intend to hold them 5 years or longer. I bonds will continue to earn tax deferred interest for 30 years. You cannot cash them in at all during the first year, and if you cash them in within the first 5 years you forfeit the last 3 months of interest. So after one year they are semi-liquid and after 5 years they are totally liquid. The base rate stays the same for the entire time you hold the bond. If you had purchased an I bond in May of 2000, your bond would still be earning a base rate of 3.6% plus the current inflation rate of .74%, for a total earnings rate of 4.34%. How would you like to be holding, right now, a 100% liquid, 100% safe investment that is paying you 4.34%? The inflation rate was as high as 2.85% back in 2005. Unfortunately, the current base rate (as of November 2014) is set at 0%. As a result, I bonds might not be a great investment right now, but once interest rates rise to 1%, 2%, or 3%, they will once again become a really interesting investment choice.

The one negative drawback to I bonds is that you cannot invest more than $10,000 per person annually, although a husband and wife can each invest up to $10,000 for the year. You can also buy them in any amount between $25 and $10,000 (and they mean that quite literally: you can invest $352.10, if desired). These bonds can only be purchased directly from the U.S. Treasury website at www.treasurydirect. gov.

Another important feature to note is that an I bond may only be redeemed in full, so I suggest that you purchase them in smaller denominations like $2,500 or $5,000. This offers you more flexibility and maintains a little tighter control on the tax consequences at a future point in time. Another advantage of I bonds is that the interest becomes tax free if spent on higher education, so they can make great gifts for younger children.

It's unfortunate that I bonds are seldom promoted, but the reason is quite obvious. Guess who earns a commission or gets paid a fee when you buy an I bond? Absolutely no one. The U.S. Treasury can't or won't advertise them, and financial advisors don't tell you about them because there is nothing in it for them. So the only people who will tell their clients about them are those who believe in true diversification and put their clients' interests first. On the other hand, this does offer you an opportunity to test your financial advisor by asking him or her what they know about I bonds and if they think I bonds have any place in your portfolio. Since after reading this chapter you will already have made up your mind as to whether or not I bonds interest you, the answer your advisor gives you should offer some insight into whether the two of you are on the same page with respect to your investments.

Chapter 7

WALL STREET

"Sometimes people don't want to hear the truth because they don't want their illusions destroyed."

--Friederich Nietzsche

The year is 2008 and Americans lost $74 billion of personal dollars of equity in their real estate and in their retirement accounts. Plus the government has to "loan" the Wall Street firms and banks $426 billion to keep them from collapsing. In addition, the government has to spend trillions to keep the economy afloat. To top all that off, the Wall Street firms pay out $17.5 billion in bonuses to themselves for doing such a great job. Then in 2009, while our whole country is in the depths of the Great Recession, they pay themselves another $22.5 billion in bonuses.

The idea behind the federal bailout was to keep the banking system solvent so that it could and would continue to loan out money and keep America's economy running. However, instead of putting the bailout money back into the economy, the banks used the money to buy their own stock. After all, they had just been informed that the government would not let them go bankrupt, so it was a no-risk investment. They also knew that once everyone else realized the banks could not fail, they would start buying the stock too, which meant the stock prices would rise and they would make money on the purchase of their own stock by selling it back to investors at the higher prices.

The TARP bill was signed by President George Bush in October 2008. Citigroup stock hit a low of 97 cents a share on May 2, 2009, having fallen from a high of $57 in December 2006. By April 2010, just one year later, the stock price was at approximately $5 per share and Citigroup paid off its interest-free loan. In addition, you must realize that Citigroup had a 1 for 10 stock split (this is called a reverse split) in May 2011. This means they traded one new stock share for 10 old ones, so overnight it looked as though the stock had jumped from $4 to $40, even though it actually wasn't worth a penny more. This whole scenario is what restarted the 5-year rally.

Before I go any further, let me say that I do love the stock market. It's the Wall Street firms I can't believe in or trust. To understand how we got here, we need to go all the way back to 1933, right after the Great Depression. The government realized that one of the major causes of the Great Depression was the collapse of the stock market and that the collapse had occurred because the banking system had allowed people to borrow exorbitant amounts of money to invest into the market. Now if you stop and think about this for a minute, you can see the problem. If you went to your neighborhood bank and asked for a $10,000 loan, and when they asked why you needed it, you said, "to invest in the stock market," they would have laughed you right out the door. But back then most of the big Main Street banks were also the big Wall Street banks, and because they knew they were going to get the money right back and also make commissions on it, they were more than happy to loan the money.

This brought about the Glass-Steagall Act, which divided the banking industry into investment and commercial banks, in other words

Main Street banks and Wall Street banks. But the big banking firms worked for decades to find ways to work around or abolish the act. Finally in 1999, they convinced Congress that it was no longer useful and were successful in having the law abolished. Eight years later we entered the Great Recession. That worked well, don't you think?

As evidence to how the commercial banks and the Main Street banks have once again basically merged, I offer you the following partial list of the top 10 Wall Street firms based on size: J.P. Morgan Chase (Chase Bank) #1, Bank of America #2, Citi #3, Wells Fargo #4, and U.S. Bank (UBS) #8. These are also the biggest players in Main Street banking, in that they sponsor credit cards, underwrite mortgages, and are huge players in checking and savings account banking.

I know one unfortunate woman who believed she had enough to retire from her well-paying job as a laboratory technician in a major brewery in 1999. Two and a half years later, after nearly half of her retirement account disappeared because of the market decline, she went back to work as a checkout clerk with a major grocery chain. Six years later, just as she was almost back to where she had been in 1999, the market took another major nose dive. Luckily, before the second downturn, she had followed some of my advice and took steps to protect about half her money. In the end she only lost about 20% of her savings and was therefore able to weather the storm. All the earnings you see on paper aren't worth anything until you turn them into real money that you can put into your pocket and spend as you see fit.

Educating yourself is, and always will be, one of the best investments you can or ever will make. There are many good ways to make money. There are stocks, bonds, mutual funds, ETFs, REITs, real estate, and managed accounts. All those ways can and do work, but they work best when you understand them and their limitations. Most of the "education," and I use that word lightly, could probably be better defined as propaganda. The reason is that most of the information is provided by those who will benefit when you invest in a particular market. The general rule of thumb to remember is that every investment, let me repeat that, every investment has positive traits and negative traits. It is your job to do one of two things.

One, you can research until you feel you know the negatives or, two, you can find someone who is willing to share that information with you. So how do you know when someone is telling you the whole story? First, if you ask them for the negatives or weak spots of a particular investment and they say there are none, I advise you to run for the door as fast as you can. Another good question to ask is, "Are bonds safe?" Most Wall Street representatives will say yes. Granted that bonds are safer than stocks, they do not meet my definition of safe. Between 1991 and 1994, bonds lost approximately 28% of their value because of a rising interest rate market. Losing 28% is not my definition of safe. As interest rates rise, bond values go down and, of course, the opposite is true. We will cover that explanation shortly.

As stated earlier, I do believe in the stock market and have been a student of it since about 1970. The most important lesson I have learned is that you cannot believe most of the propaganda that Wall Street issues. You must take the time to learn what is true and what is "noise." Noise is information that is disseminated by Wall Street to persuade you to act. They don't actually care if you believe it; so long as you act, they will make money and that is their primary goal, to take some of your money and make it theirs.

If I were trying to teach you about the stock market, I could tell you about stochastics, MACD (moving average convergence divergence), candlestick charting, what a doji is, and countless other methods that someone might use to convince you that there is a way to predict what the market is going to do next. But there is no system that can accurately predict what the market is going to do next. More importantly, that is not what this book is about. The goal is to help you stay financially intact.

So we are going to discuss in this chapter information that you can use to do exactly that. Besides explaining a lot of the investments and how to use them, I will also share with you a chart of the S&P 500, which we will use to help you understand what is true and why you can't believe a large part of what you have been taught to this point in time. I don't expect you to simply accept everything I say as gospel truth. But I will try my best to explain in detail, with logic and everyday common sense, the hows and whys of what I believe is true and accurate. All I ask is that you absorb this information and then use it to come to your own conclusions. Believe me, no one cares more about your money than you do, and when armed with good information you will make far better choices than most of the financial advisors you could ever hire.

To understand how we got where we are today, we need to return to the beginning and the basics and then work our way to present day. The first "stock markets" actually had nothing to do with stocks. Ever since the beginning of man, we have always traded goods. Somebody had too many chickens but no coat. Someone else had plenty of furs to make a coat but no chickens. Hence, they decided to trade chickens for furs. The problem was, the person with too many chickens might live in one town and the person with too many furs might live in another town and they would never meet.

Enter the traveling merchant. He would buy from one and sell to the other, keeping a little of each as payment for his time and services. Eventually, coins were invented to make the system work more efficiently. So now to become a merchant, you had to have a sufficient number of coins to establish an inventory. The choice was whether you started very small or you borrowed money (more coins) from someone else. The person you borrowed from wanted their money to make money for them, so they charged interest. The individuals who loaned money to the merchants were the beginning of the banking system. Sometimes, for one reason or another, the money lender would want to get cashed out of a deal, so he would go to his fellow "bankers" and see if one of them wanted to buy the loan from him.

The first actual "stock exchange" in America was built to trade war bonds, not company stocks. It was the work of Alexander Hamilton, serving as the first U.S. Secretary of the Treasury, and it was located at the corner of Wall Street and Broadway in New York. Stocks and stock trading came a little later. In the beginning, the way to open and run a business was by borrowing money. Then someone got the idea of offering part ownership in the company rather than borrowing money. With the lure of participating in the company's profits, they could avoid having to pay a fixed interest rate or any principal. They would still pay the new owners something for the use of their money, but now instead of calling it interest they would call it a dividend. In addition, they would be able to hold onto some of the profit and use it for growing the business, so that they wouldn't have to borrow more money or sell more shares, thereby not diluting the percentage of ownership for those who bought the stock. And the stockholders' shares would be worth more because the company's value would increase. Finally, if someone wanted to get their money out of the investment, they could sell their share of the company to someone else who wanted to buy into it. Hence, the stock market was born and should probably more aptly be called a "market of stocks."

I could write an entire chapter on the history of the market, but there are several others who have already done that quite well. If you really want to understand the mechanics of the exchanges, there are two really good books that I recommend. I must warn you, however, that once you have read these books you might never want to trade the market again, because you will truly understand just how manipulated the markets actually are. The two books are: "KING OF THE CLUB" by Charles Gasparino and "FLASH BOYS" by Michael Lewis.

Since I mentioned "manipulation," let me briefly cover why I use that word. When you look at a stock, one of the numbers you will see is something called the P/E ratio. P/E stands for price to earnings ratio. Remember earlier I mentioned the lure of profits? That's where the P/E ratio comes in. It means that if the profit related to one share of stock is $1 and the P/E ratio is 17, then the price of one share of stock is $17.

If we wanted to buy the pizza store down on the corner, we would ask to see the current owner's financial statements. Let's say after examining the books we see that last year the business turned a $50,000 profit. If Wall Street were selling this business and wanted a P/E ratio of 15, it means that you would have to pay $750,000 for that pizza parlor. The pizza parlor would have to operate at last year's level for 15 years just for you to get your money back. Now, of course, the hope is that you would be able to improve the business and make it more profitable. But would you even consider buying that pizza parlor for $750,000? If not, why then do we even consider paying that kind of premium for a publicly traded company, outside of the fact that we basically have no other choice?

This is why there is so much movement in stock prices. Not because anything has actually happened with the company, other than the perception of its future has changed. Considering perception is 90% of reality, this leaves a lot of room for manipulation and movement with no true grounds or reason. The mere fact that people think a company is going to do well over the next 6 months has no bearing on whether or not the company actually does. Of course, the opposite is also true.

Odds are that for the majority of the 8,000 companies listed on the stock exchanges, nothing major is going to happen between 4 o'clock this afternoon when the market closes and 9:30 tomorrow morning when the market opens again. Therefore, all the companies should hold almost the exact same value, yet almost every single one of them will open at a different price in the morning than where it closed at to-day. Why? Because the perception of the buying and selling public has changed. The vast majority of the news you hear is designed to change perception, because the only way that the stock markets can keep you in the game is by changing your perception. Wall Street only makes money when people are buying and selling, therefore they have to give you reasons to be buying or selling. So now that you have a basic understanding of why the markets move, let us proceed.

The basic premise of the stock market – that investing in the stock market is one of the best ways to accumulate wealth – is absolutely true and yet it is a problem. Why? Because we, as logical humans, assume that if an end result is true then all of the interim information must also be true. But that is a false assumption on our part. We have been taught for as long as I can remember that the market averages about 10% growth per year. That statement is basically true, but it is much misunderstood. When we hear those words all we see is growth. We don't stop to think why that number actually exists, and yet there is a very logical reason why approximately 10% is the magic number. That number didn't happen by accident or mere coincidence.

If you take the three basics parts of the economy, you will see that the stock market is simply mirroring what is already happening. The economy is not following the stock market, the stock market is telling us the story of the economy. The three main parts of the economy are: interest rate, inflation rate, and the GDP (Gross Domestic Product).

The average interest rate over the past 100 years has been approximately 4%. The 10-year treasury rate is 4.9%, but most of us don't buy the 10-year treasuries, we buy 6-month to 5-year CDs which pay less, averaging out to about a 4% return for the public dealing with the banking industry. The average inflation rate over the last 100 years comes in at 3.22%, and the average GDP for the last 70 years (the longest time frame I can find) has been calculated at 3.27%. When you add the three figures together you end up with right around 10%. One might say that it's merely a coincidence. However, as a student of the market and the economy for 50 years, I have very seldom found 100-year coincidences.

The saying "making money is easy, keeping it is the hard part" has never been more true than when talking about the stock market. All accounts go up and down, so controlling the losses is of utmost importance. Let's say you start with $100 and you lose 50% of your money. Do you realize that you then have to earn 100% just to get back to even? When you lose the 50% you only have $50 left, so now you have to double your money (earn 100%) to return to where you started. Another example of percentage losses: if you made 50% on your $100 you would have $150, but then if you lost 50% you would end up with

$75. So even though the gain/loss percentages were exactly the same, you ended up losing money. Understanding the basics will help you become a better investor and make you less susceptible to sales practices that do not have your best interest at heart.

Wall Street and the vast majority of everyone connected with Wall Street, which means the stockbrokers and the financial advisors in your home town, will tell you that diversification is the key to controlling losses. If they defined diversification correctly, they would be correct, but they don't. To them diversification frequently means nothing more than owning several mutual funds. There are approximately 8,000 individual stocks and about 8,000 mutual funds at present. On average, a mutual fund will own between 30 and 40 stocks. So to achieve true diversification (inside the stock market), there should only be room for about 200 mutual funds or else the funds start to become more and more alike. So the mere fact that you own several mutual funds does not obtain diversification inside the stock market, let alone true diversification.

As proof, let's look at two funds from the same mutual fund company. One fund is called a "balanced fund" and the other is called a "fundamental fund." The name of the company or the funds is not important, for you will find approximately the same results no matter where you look. On a given day, the top 10 holdings for the "balanced fund" were: Chevron, Wells Fargo, Home Depot, Berkshire Hathaway, Royal Dutch, Amazon, Merck, Goldman Sachs, Union Pacific, and American Express. The top holdings for the "fundamental fund" on that day were: Merck, Home Depot, Citi, Microsoft, Amazon, Google, Apple, Wells Fargo, Verizon, and Baxter. Even with two totally different kinds of mutual funds, we find each has 5 stocks in common.

Buying a lot of different mutual funds will not necessarily give you diversification or any measure of safety, it just makes you scattered. And if you look at any prospectus you will find that almost all mutual funds compare their results against the S&P 500, and in most cases they fall short of matching those results. One of the reasons they can't beat the index is all the trading fees associated with trying to beat the index. So my question is, why not just buy the S&P 500? This now gives you true "inside the market" diversification, because it represents every industry in our economy among the top 500 companies, with no repeats. If you want fewer companies, you can use the Dow Jones Industrial Average, and if you want more use the Russell 2000.

The indexes are efficient in that there are very few trades involved, therefore very little in trading expenses. It is also very easy to buy just the index. Some mutual fund companies offer an S&P 500 index fund or you can buy the ETF (exchange-traded fund). The stock symbol for the S&P index is SPY. At times it is called a "tracking stock," and it sells like a stock and mirrors the S&P 500, selling at almost exactly 10% of the full price of the index, which keeps it more affordable.

The S&P 500 came into existence in 1950, so its 64-year history provides us with a lot of data to analyze and learn from in regards to whether we should invest in the market, how to invest in the market, and how to know when to be in or out of the market. So starting with the raw data, I offer the following worksheet to achieve those goals.

All the numbers for this chart came from historical information you can find on Yahoo Finance. (Just for the record, Yahoo Finance is one of the better places to find a lot of basic stock market information.) From the chart we see that basically, on average, 3 out of every 4 years the market is up and 1 out of every 4 is a down year. If you were to examine the numbers more closely, as in weekly or monthly data, you would actually learn that most "up" trends last 3 ½ years to 5 years and most "down" trends last 18 months to 2 years. Tracking this trend is very important information, for it tells us that the market goes up slowly but comes down very quickly. The chart also shows us that the average up year is 13% and the average down is 13%. Therefore, a reasonable expectation of market returns can be found with simple math.

Here is an example: 3 up years at 13% compounding would equal 44% total, then we subtract the one bad year of 13%, leaving us with 31% over a 4-year period or an average of 7.75%. Now if we take the

WALL STREET

Date	Open	Close	$ change	%age change				
1/3/1950	16.66	20.77	4.11	24.67%	1		24.67	
1/2/1951	20.77	23.8	3.03	14.59%	1		14.59	
1/2/1952	23.8	26.54	2.74	11.51%	1		11.51	
1/2/1953	26.54	24.95	-1.59	-5.99%		1		5.99
1/4/1954	24.95	36.75	11.8	47.29%	1		47.29	
1/3/1955	36.75	45.16	8.41	22.88%	1		22.88	
1/3/1956	45.16	46.2	1.04	2.30%	1		2.3	
1/2/1957	46.2	40.33	-5.87	-12.71%		1		12.71
1/2/1958	40.33	55.44	15.11	37.47%	1		37.47	
1/2/1959	55.44	59.91	4.47	8.06%	1		8.06	
1/4/1960	59.91	57.57	-2.34	-3.91%		1		3.91
1/3/1961	57.57	71.55	13.98	24.28%	1		24.28	
1/2/1962	71.55	63.1	-8.45	-11.81%		1		11.81
1/2/1963	63.1	75.02	11.92	18.89%	1		18.89	
1/2/1964	75.02	84.75	9.73	12.97%	1		12.97	
1/4/1965	84.75	92.43	7.68	9.06%	1		9.06	
1/3/1966	92.43	80.33	-12.1	-13.09%		1		13.09
1/3/1967	80.33	96.47	16.14	20.09%	1		20.09	
1/2/1968	96.47	103.86	7.39	7.66%	1		7.66	
1/2/1969	103.86	92.06	-11.8	-11.36%		1		11.36
1/2/1970	92.06	92.15	0.09	0.10%	1		0.1	
1/4/1971	92.15	102.09	9.94	10.79%	1		10.79	
1/3/1972	102.09	118.06	15.97	15.64%	1		15.64	
1/2/1973	118.06	97.55	-20.51	-17.37%		1		17.37
1/2/1974	97.55	68.65	-28.9	-29.63%		1		29.63
1/2/1975	68.65	90.19	21.54	31.38%	1		31.38	
1/2/1976	90.19	107.46	17.27	19.15%	1		19.15	
1/3/1977	107.46	95.1	-12.36	-11.50%		1		11.5
1/3/1978	95.1	96.11	1.01	1.06%	1		1.06	
1/2/1979	96.11	107.94	11.83	12.31%	1		12.31	
1/2/1980	107.94	135.76	27.82	25.77%	1		25.77	
1/2/1981	135.76	122.55	-13.21	-9.73%		1		9.73
1/4/1982	122.55	140.65	18.1	14.77%	1		14.77	
1/3/1983	140.65	164.93	24.28	17.26%	1		17.26	
1/3/1984	164.93	167.2	2.27	1.38%	1		1.38	
1/2/1985	167.2	211.28	44.08	26.36%	1		26.36	
1/2/1986	211.28	242.17	30.89	14.62%	1		14.62	
1/2/1987	242.17	247.1	4.93	2.04%	1		2.04	
1/4/1988	247.1	277.72	30.62	12.39%	1		12.39	
1/3/1989	277.72	353.4	75.68	27.25%	1		27.25	
1/2/1990	353.4	330.2	-23.2	-6.56%		1		6.56
1/2/1991	330.2	417.03	86.83	26.30%	1		26.3	
1/2/1992	417.03	435.7	18.67	4.48%	1		4.48	
1/4/1993	435.7	466.51	30.81	7.07%	1		7.07	
1/3/1994	466.51	459.21	-7.3	-1.56%		1		1.56
1/3/1995	459.21	615.93	156.72	34.13%	1		34.13	
1/2/1996	615.93	740.74	124.81	20.26%	1		20.26	
1/2/1997	740.74	970.43	229.69	31.01%	1		31.01	
1/2/1998	970.43	1229.23	258.8	26.67%	1		26.67	
1/4/1999	1229.23	1469.25	240.02	19.53%	1		19.53	
1/3/2000	1469.25	1320.28	-148.97	-10.14%		1		10.14
1/2/2001	1320.28	1148.08	-172.2	-13.04%		1		13.04
1/2/2002	1148.08	879.82	-268.26	-23.37%		1		23.37
1/2/2003	879.82	1111.92	232.1	26.38%	1		26.38	
1/2/2004	1111.92	1211.92	100	8.99%	1		8.99	
1/3/2005	1211.92	1248.29	36.37	3.00%	1		3	
1/3/2006	1248.29	1418.03	169.74	13.60%	1		13.6	
1/3/2007	1418.03	1467.97	49.94	3.52%	1		3.52	
1/2/2008	1467.97	902.99	-564.98	-38.49%		1		38.49
1/2/2009	902.99	1116.56	213.57	23.65%	1		23.65	
1/4/2010	1116.56	1257.62	141.06	12.63%	1		12.63	
1/3/2011	1257.62	1258.86	1.24	0.10%	1		0.1	
1/4/2012	1258.86	1426.19	167.33	13.29%	1		13.29	
1/4/2013	1426.19	1848.36	422.17	29.60%	1		29.6	
1/2/2014	1845.86	2058.9	213.04	11.54%	1			
					49	16	798.2	220.26
							16.289796	13.76625
							average percentage up	average percentage down

S&P 500 average dividend of around 2%, we end up with 9.75% (which you might notice is very close to the 10% average return for the industry). So as I stated earlier, the basic premise that the stock market is one of the best places to accumulate wealth is absolutely true. But now comes the difference between what others teach and my financially intact philosophy.

What others have preached and taught for many years is that you stick with the market through thick and thin and you don't try to time it, because the market always goes up, and you are better to simply stick with it through the tough times until it comes back. Wall Street is right on two of those issues. It's true that you can't time the market and, so far anyway, it's true that the market always comes back. Where I disagree is staying in the market during the downturns.

My office is located on a fairly busy street and the hospital is about a mile away. So if I used the same philosophy when crossing the street as they propose you do with your investments, then I shouldn't worry about traffic when crossing the street. After all, if I get hit, the ambulance will take me to the hospital and I will most likely be okay in a couple of years. Personally, I would rather wait for the traffic to pass and then cross the street. Do I lose a little of my precious time while waiting? Of course I do, but I will still get to my destination a whole lot faster than taking the detour through the hospital. The same goes for your hard-earned investment dollars.

You will get to your destination much faster if you are willing to slow down once in a while and let the "bad times" pass you by. But it's nevertheless true that we can't time the market, and the logic for that is quite simple. Unless we are just plain lucky, we can't buy at the bottom and sell at the top, because we don't know where the top is until after it has happened, and, conversely we don't know the bottom until after it has happened. It's no different than the old adage "buy low, sell high." Have you ever had a broker tell you to sell something when it is at the top? No, they wait until the disaster has happened before advising you to give up on the investment. If we can't time the market, then the next best thing we can do is realize, as soon as possible, when the market has switched from an uptrend to a downtrend and vice versa. That little trick, believe it or not, is actually quite simple to achieve.

Professional traders use many different tools and techniques to know when to buy and when to sell. The most common and prevalent tool is one referred to as the moving averages. A moving average is measured by starting with a point in time, such as the closing price of a stock or index, then adding together all the closing prices for the specified time period, and dividing by the same number of time periods.

So, for instance, to calculate the 10-day moving average of the SPY (the tracking stock of the S&P 500), you would take the closing price each day for the last 10 days and add them together and then divide that total by 10. To calculate the "moving average," on the next day you would drop the first day's number, replace it with the new day's closing price, and divide by 10 again. When you do this day after day for many days, weeks, and months in a row, you find that you are drawing a tracking line. If the closing price keeps increasing, the line will move in an upward direction or if it is decreasing the line will move in a downward direction.

To do this yourself, visit Yahoo Finance, and up near the top left-hand side of the page you will see a little box that says "quote lookup." Inside that box enter "SPY" and wait while the next page loads. You will now see a chart on the right-hand side of the page. Under that chart you will see small numbers and letters (1d, 5d, 1m etc.). Click on the 1y and wait for the new chart to load. Once you are there, you will see a box at the top of the chart that says "+ indicator." Click on that box and a new drop-down box appears. Click on the + sign next to "simple moving average" and then click on the little pencil. Inside the next box that appears enter the number 10. You will instantly see a line appear, which is the graphical portrayal of the 10-day moving average.

A moving average can be done with any kind of time period, and there are many software products that can accomplish this task. Day traders use trends that last for minutes only, producing 10-minute or 20-minute moving averages, for example. Someone who trades on a daily basis but not many times a day might use something like the 10-day moving average. The longer the time period chosen, the smoother the line. However, most people are not into micro-managing their accounts; they just want to avoid the big downturns.

From the big chart of numbers, a couple of pages back, showing the 62 year history of the S&P 500, we know that we need to be invested in the market about 75% of the time. We also know that we cannot predict the future, so we can't know when the market is going to go up or down. However, we can react to what the market is telling us, and that's what I am about to show you now. Go back to the chart. At the top of it you see little boxes (1d, 5d etc.). This time click on "max." A new chart pops up showing the history of the market all the way back to shortly before 1995. Now go back to the indicator box and click on it again, and then change the moving average from 10 to 20. Because we have changed the time frame, the moving average has changed from days to months. So we are now looking at the average for the past 20 months, or the equivalent of a 200-day moving average. (If you use a different software product, you will want to use the 200-day option, because it shows the turn a little earlier).

Looking at this chart, how much would you like to have known to get out of the market in early 2000, just shortly after the blue line crossed down through the moving average line? Also, how much would you have liked knowing that it was time to get back in the market around April 2003, when the market rose above the moving average? As you can see, the moving average over a longer time period keeps you in the market for the majority of the up trends and has you out of the market for the majority of the down trends. Professional traders have a saying that really drives the point home: "The trend is our friend." We will never buy at the bottom and we will never sell at the top using this strategy, but we will participate in most of the gains and miss most of the downward moves.

The point is not whether you use the 200-day, the 20-month, the 10-month, or a 50-day moving average (though don't go over 250). But if you develop a plan and stick to it, you will be better off in the long run. You cannot second guess the plan and you cannot start thinking that maybe you can predict what's coming next. You can use any moving average you choose, although the shorter the average the more you will find yourself moving in and out of the market, which usually costs money. This method works on any individual stock, mutual fund, index, or ETF, although I tend to use a shorter moving average for individual stocks, such as a 50-day moving average.

In general, when it comes to mutual funds or even most ETFs, I believe it is best to stick with the S&P 500 for the reasons discussed earlier. On the other hand, once in a while it can be fun to try one of the high flying stocks. Wouldn't it have been grand to own stocks like Krispy Kreme or Crocs and actually know when the party was over rather than having stuck with them all the way back down? Or wouldn't it have been nice to know it was time to get out of gold when it was still at $1,600 an ounce instead of riding it all the way back down to $1,200? If you were tracking the 200-day moving average of gold (GLD), you would have known to buy around October 2008 when the price was around $800 an ounce and to sell around January 2013 when it was around $1,600 an ounce, already down from its $1,800 an ounce high.

I will post on my website, www.financiallyintact.com, when the SPY moves across the 200-day moving average. There, you can join the texting club that sends you a text whenever I post a new notice on the website. So let us now move on to some other Wall Street issues that still need to be considered in order to stay financially intact.

Outside of stocks and mutual funds, bonds are the most common form of investment sold. If you hold bonds to maturity they are safer than stocks. However, it is important to note that bonds are not truly safe and you can lose substantial amounts of money in the bond market. The bond market is directly tied to interest rates, for that is how you are rewarded for investing in bonds. The basic concept to understand is that bond values go up when interest rates are going down and bond values go down when interest rates are climbing. The best way to explain this relationship is as follows.

Let's say you own a bond that is paying 2% and two years from now new bonds are paying 4%. If you wanted to liquidate your bond, no one would be willing to buy yours at full price because they could buy a new one that is paying twice the interest. So the only way that you would be able to sell your bond would be to discount the price to where the buyer is earning the equivalent of the new bonds. At first glance one might think that's not so bad, because if you had a $100 bond that matures one year from now you would only lose 2%. But most bonds do not mature in 1 year. More typically they mature in 7 years, or 10 years, or as much as 30 years.

To keep the math simple, multiply that 2% by the number of years left to maturity of the bond and that's how much you would have to discount your bond in order to sell it. In other words if your bond wasn't going to mature for another 10 years, you would have to discount your bond by at least 20%. So now I ask you, is losing 20% of your principal your definition of safe? Of course, the inverse is also true. As interest rates fall, higher interest rate bonds gain value. How much would you pay right now for an old bond that is paying out at a 6% rate? Would you be willing to give up, say, half of that return, netting you a 3% yield, which is still better than the less than 1% we are averaging in banks right now? Most likely you would.

Now considering we are at historically low interest rates, and have been for quite some time, this will be the next crash that we see. Once the interest rates start rising, there will be a huge exodus out of the low paying bonds currently out there, and consequently there will not be a long line of people waiting to buy the low interest rate bonds, so the discounts will be huge. Watch the interest rates closely, because once they start moving up you will want to get out of the bond market as quickly as possible. The only exceptions to this rule are government EE and I bonds, and that is because the U.S. government is a ready buyer that will pay you full face value.

Although I have made my views clear about most mutual funds, I realize there are times when you have no other choice than mutual funds. Almost all monies that are in 401Ks are in mutual funds, and some people are growing their money with smaller, consistent deposits that make mutual funds a good choice. Most financial advisors sell mutual funds because they are not fully licensed to sell individual stocks or ETFs. This makes it easy for them, because they don't really have to know when to invest in different stocks. They just have to sell the concept that another professional money manager is doing all the buying and selling within the fund. They don't need to know much about the market at all, they just need to know how to sell. So mutual funds come in many shapes and sizes with a variety of fees. Some are full commission and others are no load, although no load is somewhat of a misnomer in that they still have fees but you don't pay a commission to get in or out of the fund.

So you will find two kinds of financial advisors: those who sell the funds that have a commission charge, which is how they make their money, and those who charge you a percentage as a management fee and then purchase no load funds. In either case, you still need to pay attention to your money and have some say as to when you should or shouldn't be participating in the market. Hopefully, this chapter will have provided you with the information you need to make knowledgeable decisions.

Mutual funds are, however, the reason ETFs have come about and why they are gaining popularity. We have had the basic ones for quite some time now, such as the SPY (S&P 500), the DIA (Dow Industrial Average), and the QQQ (the Nasdaq 100). When mutual funds became extremely prevalent, Wall Street found that investors were spending more with the big mutual fund companies and buying fewer individual stocks. Since financial advisors can't earn as high commissions selling in big lots to the mutual fund companies as they can to individual investors, they found their earnings were going down and so they had to find a way to bring the individual investor back to buying directly from them. The result was ETFs.

They are like miniature mutual funds in that they represent a basket of stocks, but in this case they are all related to each other by industry. Some examples are XLF, which is the banking sector exchange-traded fund made up entirely of bank stocks, or the XLE, which is the ETF for the energy sector. There are now hundreds of ETFs in all kinds of sector-specific investments.

My feelings about them are just like mutual funds. Stick with the basics, such as the SPY (S&P 500). Definitely stay away from the "multiple factor" ETFs unless you really like to gamble, because they frequently cannot produce the high returns they advertise. Stick to the basics, stay patient and consistent, and protect yourself from the downturns and you will do just fine.

I'd like to finish this chapter with these thoughts. The SEC (Securities and Exchange Commission) and FINRA (Financial Industry Regulatory Authority) are supposedly the watch dogs of the financial industry and proclaim to protect the public. I have never found that to be actually true. Let's take for example when they decided to basically eliminate what were known to be "B shares" from mutual funds.

Some time ago, loaded mutual funds were sold in 3 forms: A shares, B shares, and C shares. "A" shares meant that you paid a commission up front and then had lower yearly fees. With "B" shares you did not pay a commission up front, but you did have higher fees for a number of years and then they would convert to "A" shares. If you didn't hold onto the asset long enough, on the back end you paid the remainder of the commission not yet compensated. With "C" shares you never paid a commission but you paid the highest of fees for as long as you held the fund.

So several years ago the regulators, in their infinite wisdom, decided that "B" shares were too expensive for the "people" and decided to make it almost impossible for them to be sold. It's only my opinion, but I think the mutual fund companies decided they would rather always have their money up front, because they had to pay the commissions up front whether or not the salesperson sold "A" or "B" shares. So at their request the regulating agencies changed the rules.

In my opinion, "B" shares were an excellent choice. Many times when you first invest you don't know how long you are going to hold an investment, so why not pay the commission at the end if you don't hold it for the required length of time? According to the regulating agencies' way of thinking, we should pay a commission to buy bank CDs instead of having early withdrawal penalties for taking our money out early. This is just one example of how what they say and what they mean are two different things.

And how about Bernie Madoff? You can find books and stories on the internet where people say they started asking the regulating agencies to look into him as far back as 1999. How did the SEC allow the big banks to wiggle their way around the rules and get really bad mortgage bonds insured and sold as "A" rated investments, which caused the Great Recession? The regulating industry is there to help Wall Street control the salespersons. They don't really care what Wall Street does to you. As stated throughout this book, the only one who really cares about your money is you, and no one will ever worker harder to protect it than you.

The key to making money in the market is to avoid having to re-make the same money over and over again. You need to protect your earnings so that when the next opportunity comes along you have most of your money intact.

Chapter 8

REAL ESTATE

"Buy land. They ain't making any more of the stuff."

WILL ROGERS

R eal estate is the last of the four core areas of true diversification. We should view real estate as our primary lesson in personal financial planning, for it can teach us patience and consistency. Our home usually becomes the largest or second largest asset we own when we get to retirement. Considering all the interest we pay over the years, we barely break even or at best only end up with a little more than we paid into it, and yet real estate nevertheless remains one of our greatest assets.

I once had a great teacher who was teaching finance classes to financial professionals. One day he asked our opinions about the best way to accumulate money. We each gave our biased answers and at the end he told us we were all wrong and that he was willing to argue the fact after we heard his answer, if we didn't agree that he was right. His scenario went as follows. If you took 10% of everything you made from your very first dollar and put it in a hole in the ground in your backyard and then put a bear trap over the hole, where would you have the most money when you retired, considering all your investments? We all had to admit our greatest asset most likely would be the money in the hole in the ground. His point was that growth is not our greatest challenge, holding onto our money is.

Home ownership teaches most of us this lesson. We buy our houses, we pay interest on them for 30 years in most cases, and then we end up with one huge asset. We didn't earn a penny of interest on our investment and instead paid interest, yet the inflationary growth of our asset replaced what we paid out and we end up with all our money back and, often times, a little bit more. This gives us lesson number one when it comes to real estate. Whenever you refinance to get a lower interest rate, do not choose a new 30-year mortgage. If you have already paid on your current mortgage for 5 years, get a 25-year mortgage or less. In the early years of a mortgage, the greatest amount of the payment goes to interest, not to principal. So don't keep paying the same interest over and over again.

Other financial professionals may tell you that you should always have a mortgage so that you can leverage your money and not lose the tax benefits. There are three things wrong with that advice. First, the interest deduction is not anywhere near as great as it seems to be. If you are a married couple, the standard deduction is now over $12,000, so if your mortgage interest plus property taxes and other deductions add up to $16,000, the only extra benefit you are getting from the tax deduction is $4,000. If you are in a 25% tax bracket, then your benefit is about $1,000, but you paid out approximately $12,000 in interest to get that benefit. I would rather pay taxes than interest any day of the week.

The second thing wrong with the advice is that most people do not leverage the tax benefit and make more money with it. Instead, they spend it. The only way that leveraging works is when you take money out of one house and invest it in another piece of property that you rent out. In this way you use a little bit of your money and have someone else (the renters) making the payments on the property, but since you own it you earn the appreciation of the property. That is true leveraging.

The third thing wrong with the advice is that the best thing you can do for yourself at retirement is to have no mortgage. It's a lot easier to retire comfortably if you have no debts. Also, it lessens the effect of inflation on your retirement savings if you don't have to spend a lot of those savings on interest payments. By the time you retire you need to be earning interest, not paying it.

Beyond owning your own home, there are other ways to be diversified into real estate. The obvious, of course, is owning rental properties, and I have known a lot of clients who have become quite wealthy doing just that. But being a landlord isn't for everybody. I never wanted to be a landlord, and I know a lot of people don't have enough money to get started along those lines, but fortunately there is another way to participate in real estate without actually owning buildings or land.

There are investments inside the stock market called REITs (Real Estate Investment Trusts). They sell in shares like a stock and are very liquid -- unlike any other real estate investment. They are also like an exchange-traded fund (ETF) or mutual fund in that a REIT holds several properties, which helps with the safety of the investment. By law, a REIT has to pay out 90% of its taxable income to the owners to stay qualified as a REIT. The law was signed by President Dwight Eisenhower in 1960 so that everyday Americans could participate in the advantages of investing in real estate and yet to this day, over 50 years later, most Americans still don't have any of their investable assets in this class.

REITs have come a long way since 1960. There is a great website where you can learn a lot more about REITs and the different types you can buy. To learn more visit www.reit.com. With a REIT you can buy and manage commercial properties, or just residential properties, or just leisure-type properties, or my current favorite, health care properties. I currently like that group of REITs because of America's current demographics. With all the baby boomers now aging and entering retirement, I see a great need for health care properties, such as assisted-living homes.

Of course, REITs took a big hit when the entire sector of the economy collapsed, but on average REITs hold their value pretty well and pay out reasonable dividends. Many of the bigger, more established REITs pay a dividend in the 4% range, sometimes a little more. Just like any other investment, their value does go up and down, so you can use a moving average to decide when to be invested in a REIT and when not to be, just like any other stock. That is the true beauty of participating in real estate through REITs. You can earn a reasonable return and participate in the real estate market in a totally liquid fashion, and you can do it with small amounts of money.

REVERSE MORTGAGES

Before moving on from the topic of real estate, we need to discuss one area of it that has been seriously abused. Reverse mortgages, like any other investment, can be a helpful tool when used correctly and under the correct circumstances. However, even though people have to meet with a HUD counselor before entering into a reverse mortgage, they are still being seriously abused. It is a great way for banks and banking institutions to buy your property back from you for a fraction of the price.

The idea was a good one when reverse mortgages were first established. Many people wanted to stay in their homes but simply couldn't afford to for one reason or another. A reverse mortgage can sometimes be the right thing to do when people run out of other options to stay in their homes and when it makes no sense to sell the home and pay rent somewhere else. I have actually advised people to do a reverse mortgage, but I have probably done that only 3 times in the past 20 years.

The government passed a law in 1987 that allowed these mortgages to be insured. The first varieties started about 20 years before that, but they didn't gain much popularity until the 1987 law. The problem comes in how they are marketed. I have clients who have a couple hundred thousand dollars in the bank asking me if they should get a reverse mortgage. It is not an investment product. Money should not be "borrowed" out of your home just to invest somewhere else that might give you a better return than the interest you are paying on the loan or to provide you with an income that you cannot outlive. Yet many times this is exactly how reverse mortgages are marketed.

And lately the ads very seldom call the program a reverse mortgage. Instead they refer to "a new government program" called an HECM, which allows people to increase their monthly income. I know this because I am over 62 and get these ads in the mail. Now, of course, I know to look hard to see if the ad ever refers to the program by its most common name of reverse mortgage. Sometimes you can find that term in the fine print.

The best way to use a reverse mortgage, if you find yourself in that position, is to take no more money out of the house than you need and not before it is actually needed. Some salespeople encourage you to take out (borrow) more than needed, or even the entire amount allowed, and then suggest you reinvest that money. This is a terrible idea. Interest starts to accrue from the day you take the money out, and that interest will eat up the remaining equity in the home. So if all you need is $1,000 a month, only take out a $1,000 a month. That way, at the end of the year you are only accruing interest on $12,000. If you took out $100,000 you would have accrued interest on $100,000. At a 6% interest rate, in the first scenario you have only used up about $600 of additional equity, but in the second scenario you have used up $6,000 of equity with nothing to show for it. Make sure you seek good, unbiased advice if you are considering a reverse mortgage.

Real estate, like the other areas of my C.A.S.H. system, can help you stay financially intact when used wisely.

Chapter 9

THE DOGGIE BAG

You know how sometimes you go out and have a nice meal but it's a little more than you can handle, so you take the remainder home to have something to chew on later? Well, that describes this last chapter of the book. There are a few remaining issues I wanted to cover and either because they didn't fit well into one of the other chapters or simply because I wanted to leave you with a little something to chew on, I decided to put them in this chapter.

So let's start with a little test. Here is a French word: "avertisse-ment." Do you know how it translates into English? And the Spanish word: "advertencia." Do you know what it means in English? I'm betting most people would guess that both of those words translate into the English word "advertisement," but that would be incorrect. Both the French and the Spanish words translate into the English word "warning."

Whatever happened to the saying "buyer beware"? I remember as a young man you would hear that phrase on a fairly regular basis or its Latin equivalent, "caveat emptor." It's probably even more important now, and yet we rarely hear this phrase anymore. Whatever happened to "truth in advertising"? According to the Federal Trade Commission it still exists, but I seriously question to what extent. According to the Commission's website, "when the FTC finds a case of fraud perpetrated on consumers, the agency files actions in federal district court for immediate and permanent orders to stop scams; prevent fraudsters from perpetrating scams in the future; freeze their assets; and get compensation for victims."

Deception and fraud are not necessarily the same thing. Deception can be either a "little" misleading, "moderately" misleading, or an outright lie. The outright lies get labeled as scams, and those seem to be the only ones that the FTC addresses once they are brought to its attention. Now don't get me wrong. I am definitely not for big government -- it's already too big -- but consumer laws are too weak and enforcement is even weaker.

On the other hand we Americans, to a great extent, have to accept the blame for letting things get as out of hand as they have. We are lied to on daily basis. We are lied to so much that we actually expect it to happen and therefore let it happen. Because we are consistently and constantly lied to, we have become somewhat calloused to it. Because we accept little lies on a daily basis, it becomes easier and easier for us to become somewhat gullible to the bigger lies. We are lied to by our corporations, Wall Street, and even our government. Let me give you a couple of examples of little lies that we accept as normal.

Have you ever noticed that most times when you call a major corporation you hear, "Your call is very important to us, but due to unexpected heavier than normal call volume we have to put you on hold"? You can call the minute they open, or any other minute of the day, and get the exact same message. Most of these corporations have been in existence for decades. Do you really believe they don't know what their average daily call volume is? So one of two lies has just been told to us. They are either lying about the unexpected call volume or they are lying about caring about our call. I would actually appreciate it if a corporation's voice message was honest, like, "In order to keep our prices low, we staff our call center with just enough people that the average wait should be less than 10 minutes. Thank you for understanding." Wouldn't that be a refreshing change?

Wall Street lies to us too. Recently, a Wall Street report claimed on one day that the stock market was up because people were happy that the price of oil was going down, which meant cheaper gasoline prices. The very next day, the market was lower because the price of oil was down and investors were worrying about people in the oil industry losing their jobs. As I stated in Chapter 7, Wall Street wants movement in the market and so it will spin the news to create just that.

While on the subject of spinning the news, the government is among the all-time champions. You need to look no further than the so-called published inflation rate or the unemployment rate. The government doesn't lie, it just changes the definitions to make the figures match the desired results. As stated in an earlier chapter, how is it that the economy is too weak to raise interest rates, so that senior citizens can make enough to keep up with inflation, yet the stock market is hitting all-time highs? All-time highs means corporate America in general is apparently doing great, so where is this weakness they report? It doesn't exist. If we allow everyone to keep lying to us with no consequence, then I suppose we deserve what we get. We need to start holding all these people responsible for their actions and what they say.

MEGA MILLIONS LOTTERY
While I think lotteries are a great sham, I actually have mixed feelings about them. All lotteries are a form of self-taxation, and it's a lot more of a tax than you may realize, but we will get to that in a minute. I personally think lotteries hurt the economy more than they help and people are better off not playing them. On the other hand, they do help keep taxes down, so in that sense I am fine with other people voluntarily paying part of my tax bill for me. But here's why I think they are a sham. You will have to forgive me for going into accountant mode, but it is necessary. I won't bore you with all the math, just enough to make the point.

The governmental agencies claim that about half the lottery money goes to prizes and half is spent on various specific programs (depending on which state you live in). In reality the government gets a whole lot more than half of the proceeds, and much of that does not go to the programs you think you are indirectly helping. The math looks like this. The odds of winning the jackpot are 1 in 258,890,850. The minor prize amounts stay consistent, no matter how big the jackpot gets, and we know the odds of winning any of the minor prizes. For example, we know that in 258,890,850 tickets there will be approximately 885,315 $5 winners. Because 50% goes to prizes, once that many tickets have been sold all the minor prizes put together will total only $31,408,310. That leaves $98,445,425 for the major prizes.

We also know there will be 14 $1 million winners. We subtract that from the $98 million and end up with a jackpot of $84,445,000 (they round off to the nearest $5,000). Once someone wins a million dollars or more, the federal government will get back about 38% of that in taxes (33% on the $1 million winners and 39% on the $84 million winner), and depending on the state there could be another 5% average that is owed. When you put all these numbers together, you end up with total ticket sales of $258,890,850 and total taxes paid of $166,545,425 (½ of sales plus 33% on $14 million plus 39% on $84 million), and that's not counting anything for those states that assess a state income tax too. That's 62% so far. And while at least 10% to 15% goes to running the program, we are not done yet.

Let's say the person who won the jackpot goes nuts and spends $34 million before they die. That means they will leave in cash and assets about $50 million to their heirs. Guess what? Anything over $5 million gets hit again with the estate tax, which is another 40%, so in this case another $20 million in taxes, which takes us to a grand total of 72% of all the money collected in the game went back to the government in the form of taxes. So I ask you, if the government announced a lottery where every ticket was a winner but all you would win for your dollar bet was 28 cents and you didn't get your dollar back, would you play? Collectively, that is exactly what is happening. If you want to gamble, go to a casino. The worst machines on the floor still pay back at least

80%, and most of them quite a bit better than that. But even 80% is a far favorable game to the 27% payback of the lottery.

IS IT A CRIME AND, IF SO, WHERE WAS IT COMMITTED?

If you send money to someone as a gift, when they have not promised anything to you in return, is that a crime? Take, for instance, this story a woman told me. She had met someone through an internet dating site. The person lived in another state and was a single parent (supposedly). After a period of time (not very long), he ran into hard times and needed money to keep a roof over his family's head and food on the table. So this woman, well-educated and successful in her profession, sent him a couple thousand dollars. But once she caught on that she was being "scammed," she went to the local police department. There, she learned it is not a crime to ask for money. Since nothing had been promised in return, it was no more than a request for money. I have heard similar stories and find that it's a good question. If someone lies to you and then asks for money, is it a crime? Furthermore, if it is a crime, where did it take place? Was the crime committed in the state where the scammer lives or in the state where the victim lives, or both?

In this instance, the woman next called the FBI and was told that they only pursue cases that involve more than $50,000. So in frustration, she started to do some investigating on her own. She found that this man, or least the picture of the man, was actually on several dating sites, but he had a different name and a different profile on each of the sites. This led her to believe that he was scamming several people and she called the FBI back with this information, along with where he lived, etc. This time someone took interest in her story and started to work with her. However, the FBI agent told her that the first thing she had to do was file a report with her local police department. Her local police department still did not want to file a report on her behalf, so she requested a report form, filled it out herself, and then asked them to sign it. Eventually she won this battle. All in all it is turning out to be a good thing, because they have discovered thus far that the man is taking the money from the U.S. to another country, and eventually the money is being funneled to a militant group in Africa.

Our law enforcement agencies, as much as I respect them, have to do a better job of educating the public about how to handle these cases and what has to occur before they can help us. In this particular case, I know if the woman had called our state's Bureau of Investigation first they would have been able to help her right from the beginning. So I leave you with this thought. If your local police department can't help you for one reason or another, your next call should be to your own state's Bureau of Investigation and ask for the victim advocates department.

A COUPLE OF OTHER THINGS

A few other things are not scams or shams, but they cost us money both personally and as a society in general. A couple examples are air miles and cash back cards. For a few people these actually provide a benefit, but it is a very small percentage of the population. The worst part about them is that they cost everyone money, yet very few people benefit. When merchants take a card as payment, they have to pay fees to several entities, including the card company, the bank that issued the card, and the processor. Fees on credit cards are higher than those on debit cards, and fees on cash back or air miles cards are higher still. As much as credit companies like to promote the cards, they are one of those things that sound really good but offer very little benefit.

I found several sites on the internet that reported as much as 75% of the miles never get claimed or used and up to another 20% take as long as five years to be redeemed. Part of that reason, of course, is due to how long it takes a person to accumulate enough miles (reward) to use. The card companies push the use of these options because it gets consumers to stay with them longer. Rather than have people chase a lower interest rate, the banks issuing the cards want to keep the accounts they acquire, and thus rewards programs were created to build customer loyalty. Obviously, the air miles program keeps us connected for the longest period of time, because we cannot "cash" it out like the other reward cards. We have to wait until we have enough points to use on travel.

The reason I say these cards are bad for the economy as a whole is because extra fees are involved. The part of the system that pays those fees is the retailer, the provider of the product or service you are purchasing with that card. The provider is not going to absorb that fee and make less profit, they are going to count that as part of the cost of business and, therefore, build that cost into the price of the product or service. As a result, everybody is helping a few people get a "reduced rate" vacation. This makes everything a little bit more expensive, and those numbers really add up. Let's say an average family buys $40,000 per year of goods and services, and let's assume that everything is marked up ½ of 1 percent just to cover the higher fees for the "rewards" cards. That means every single household in America is paying an extra $200 per year, and the vast majority of those people are getting absolutely nothing for their money. Since we have approximately 134 million households in America, that adds up to a whopping $26 billion per year. Who gets a large percentage of that money leads us into the next section.

CREDIT CARD COMPANIES AND CURRENT INTEREST RATES

Why is it that the interest rates banks pay are at all-time lows, less than 1% in most cases and frequently even less, and yet credit card interest rates are higher than they were before the big meltdown? Before the Great Recession I was getting offers all the time for 9.9% interest rate credit cards and now the best I see, on average, is about 13%. I did a quick search for best rates and only found one at 10.99% and a couple at 12.99%; all the rest ranged from 13.99% to 24.99% and that was under a "best rates" search. It is the same banks who don't want to pay us anything on our savings, it is the same banks who caused the Great Recession because of their greed, and it is the same banks that now offer air miles cards that collect extra fees for something that doesn't get used 75% of the time.

The federal bailout was supposedly to help the banks so that they could loan money to consumers and keep our economy alive. Yet when it comes to loaning money to us in the most common form that people borrow, they choose to charge us more. How is that stimulating the economy? They pay almost nothing for the funds they are using and yet they somehow think it is right to charge us more, as if we were the ones who caused the recession. I highly recommend that, whenever possible, you use the smaller, locally owned banks. They deserve your business a lot more than the nationwide firms, and many times they are the ones that pay a little bit better interest rates or offer lower rates on credit cards. Also, local banks tend to loan more money to people and businesses in their area.

ROBO CALLS

Robo calls are one of those things that should be illegal. You know the ones where your phone rings and then the next sound you hear is "click"? Why is it that these "businesses," and I use that term loosely, think that the time of their low-paid telemarketers is worth more than our time? It should be a law that if you call someone you must have a live person on the other end when the connection is made. Besides the fact that these calls are extremely annoying, they are counterproductive to the rest of the economy. I do get some robo calls at home, but I get a lot more at the office. The only ones worse than those that go "click" are the ones with an automated message. We are almost obligated to listen to the whole message just so that we can hear what number to push at the end to get removed from their list. I think it would be safe to say that my office gets about 5 of these calls a day, and it wastes about 2 minutes of our time. According to smallbusinessnotes.com, there are approximately 24.7 million small businesses in America. So if all of us are getting these calls, it equals 49.4 million wasted minutes per day. Even if we value those minutes at the minimum wage of $7.25 an hour, robo calls are sucking $5,969,166 of productivity out of our economy every day. I would have an extremely tough time believing that these services are selling anywhere near that amount on a daily basis. They are usually selling security systems, auto warranties, "low cost" loans, or Google ads (it's not really Google, but it is firms that help you buy Google ads so they are allowed to use the name). If you try to call back these numbers after the "click," you get busy signals or messages saying the number is not available or is disconnected. How can it be disconnected when it just called me? I would ask why our lawmakers can't do something about this huge waste of resources, but that opens a new subject.

POLITICAL WASTE

It's probably too much to ask Congress to pass any kind of useful law, considering they haven't even been able to pass a budget since 2009. But I think I have figured out why that is such a tough project for them: they are math challenged. When you look inside the IRS regulations, you see that if you are supposed to send in quarterly payments, you send the first one April 15, the second one June 15, the third one September 15 and the last one January 15 of the following year. That means our quarters consist of 3 months, then 2 months, then 3 months and then 4 months. See the problem? They are math challenged.

However, this does bring up my favorite political saying: "If con is the opposite of pro, is Congress the opposite of progress?" The fact that they are not doing their jobs is bad enough, but then consider that each Congressional representative, all 435 of them, are allowed to have staffs as large as 18 people with a minimum budget of $748,312, and senators each have a staff budget of at least $1,685,301. Almost a half a billion dollars a year in salaries and they can't pass a budget, can't pass a bill concerning immigration, and can't overhaul the tax codes. So why do they need those huge staffs to accomplish basically nothing? What we need is a new Constitutional amendment that states, "Any senator or congressman who is in office in a year that a budget is not passed cannot run for re-election." I bet they would find a way to get the job done then.

THE ABSOLUTE BEST WAY TO ACCUMULATE WEALTH

The short answer to accumulating wealth is to control debt. The less you borrow over your lifetime and the less interest you pay over your lifetime, the better the chances are that you will end up with more money in the end. We covered in an earlier chapter how it is actually better to pay taxes than interest. So if that is true, and it is, then what does that say about interest that brings you no benefit whatsoever? Besides the benefit of ending up with more money in your pocket, having less open credit also means there are fewer ways that identity thieves can harm you. I've been saying it for 30 years: the best way to accumulate wealth is by keeping your money in your own pocket.

FINAL TIDBITS

I would like to end this book on a positive note by leaving you with a couple of hints and methods to help protect yourself from those who wish to make your money their money. If you strive to know more about investing and all the choices that are available to you, I would highly recommend that you attend the Money Show at least once. It is a large, three-day expo full of presentations and is held every May in Las Vegas. You can learn about stocks, bonds, mutual funds, trading strategies, commodities, precious metals, oil, and the Forex (trading foreign currencies). I have gone several times and have learned a lot every time. You will hear a lot of propaganda, but you will also walk away with a whole lot of information.

I once took my oldest son and he asked me, "How do we know which parts are good information and which parts are propaganda?" An excellent question, and my answer was that we listen to all of it, but what you begin to notice is that certain concepts keep popping up. For instance, if everybody is talking about the 50-day moving average, then you know that it holds a lot of credibility. Here's another good tip: after attending a particular presentation, go to the exhibit hall and visit the booths of the speaker's competitors and see what they say. The concepts they all agree upon will ring true, the rest of it you have to take with a grain of salt and decide for yourself. You can literally stuff about 24 hours of education into 3 days, and since the majority of it is free, it is definitely worth your time and travel. On your first trip I would recommend attending only the free presentations. The sessions you have to pay for are really for the specialists, or those who wish to become specialists.

One caveat: do not believe after your first trip that you can immediately start amassing a fortune. What you will learn at the expo is just scratching the surface, and it will get you started in the right direction. You can find all the information you need at www.moneyshow.com. They also offer a couple of other shows around the country, which they sometimes call traders shows. I cannot speak for those because I have only attended the Las Vegas show.

I do know that education will never hurt you. There are two websites I use a lot when trying to figure out if information that I have seen or read is accurate or not. There are a lot of emails that catch fire because they incite a lot of emotion. They are not really scamming or shamming you, but they usually try to hurt a third party. The first source I turn to is Snopes at www.snopes.com. This site does an excellent job of tracking down the truth and even the history of where the stories come from. It's actually astonishing the truths you can learn when researching something that is untrue. The second site I feel I can trust is www.ripoff.com. It differs from Snopes in that you get a lot of opinions from everyday people. It is not uncommon to find people who will boast the virtues of a particular business while others will tell you it's the worst business on earth. Seeing both sides of any issue or question is always enlightening. I have always preached that there are two sides to every coin. It doesn't mean that one side is good and the other is bad, it's simply that one side lists the strengths and the other side features the weaknesses

The last website to mention, of course, is the one that runs in conjunction with this book: www.financiallyintact.com. On that site you will find updated blogs on new scams and old ones that have resurfaced to make another run at our money. You will also find information about seminars or workshops that I offer as well as other valuable information. I hope you find that the information contained in this book helps keep you financially intact.

EPILOGUE

I am proud to be an American. I even have a tattoo on my left arm that reads, "Made in the U.S.A," adorned with a flag. I started chapter one stating "America is us." I believe in the people, I believe in our form of government, I believe in the concept. America is a concept that lives in our hearts, our minds, and our very souls. We truly believe that "all people are created equal" and that we do have certain inalienable rights such as "life, liberty and the pursuit of happiness." But we are in trouble, and it is getting worse every day. We are under attack from the outside and the inside.

Many countries and people don't like us, but I honestly believe it is more a case of jealousy. If other nations would simply follow our lead by treating all people fairly and by educating all their citizens, they could accomplish just as much as we do and have done. You cannot treat your female population as second class citizens without throwing away half of your potential. The worst part about our enemies is that they are running many of the scams, taking our money, and then using those same funds to hurt us.

But we are also in trouble from within. Our system cannot survive, let alone flourish, when only half the population is footing the bill for the entire nation. Now don't get me wrong; I don't think we need to have the poor pay more taxes out of what they have, but we do need to help raise them to a level where they can help pay their own way. Our poor don't need more handouts, they need a hand up. We say we are the land of opportunity, yet we have developed a system that discourages the poor from seeking those opportunities. Under our current welfare system, if a recipient makes just $10 too much in one month, we cut them off at the knees and take all their benefits away. If you were a single mom and knew that if you made $10 too much you were going to lose thousands of dollars in benefits, wouldn't you be sure not to make that extra $10? We need a graduated welfare system, where if someone makes $100 too much they only lose $50 of benefits. We are a great country, but we could be better and we should be better.

It can be done, and I know it from personal experience. Several years ago I hired a young woman who was a single mom. She worked hard at a lousy job and was a welfare recipient. She was feisty but had a very pleasing personality; she was not very well educated but had an inner fire to learn. She had a really rough start but was brave enough and smart enough to remove herself from those circumstances. I knew almost as soon as I met her that all she needed was an opportunity and someone to believe in her even more than she believed in herself at the time. Today she is an office manager and has become part of the 53% of the people who are paying almost all the nation's taxes. I believe that this would be true of more welfare recipients than not if we would simply give them the chance. Poor people are not immune to scams and shams; in fact, probably just the opposite is true. They want so badly to have a better life that they will take chances and jump at what looks like a good opportunity, all in the hopes of giving their kids a better life.

We are a great country, but we could be better if we would work at raising the bar for our entire population. Being able to stay financially intact ourselves won't be worth a plug nickel if our country doesn't stay financially intact. So I ask this favor of you. If you found this book to be of value to you, please share it with your friends, family, and neighbors and let's move as an entire country towards staying FINANCIALLY INTACT.

AUTHOR BIOGRAPHY

R on Vejrostek graduated from the University of Northern Colorado in 1973 with a degree in business administration and management. In 1980, he began preparing taxes part-time, and in 1992 he moved into tax preparation and personal financial consulting full-time, acquiring the Vejrostek Tax and Financial business name in 1999. Over the last twenty-three years, he has helped thousands of people save thousands of dollars in taxes and shown those people how to keep their money safe and their nest eggs in tact. He is a Jaycees International Senator and was a founding member of the Longmont Community Foundation.

Vejrostek is also the author of Windows of Misopportunity, published in 1995.

Made in the USA
San Bernardino, CA
26 March 2018